THE VILLAGE OF

Aspects of Colern

Presented to David Coates with
gratitude and affection from
the members of Colerne Parish Church.

August 1981.

THE VILLAGE ON THE HILL

Aspects of Colerne History

Edited by
Andrew Langley and John Utting

Colerne History Group
1990

First published in 1990 by
  Colerne History Group
  c/o Colerne Parish Council
  Council Offices, Market Place, Colerne
  Chippenham, Wiltshire SN14 8DF

Reprinted, 1991

Cover design by
  William Knight and Marian Whipp

Filmset in Monophoto Plantin by
  Bath Typesetting Limited
  London Road, Bath, Avon, BA1 5NL

Printed in Great Britain by
  Antony Rowe Limited
  Bumpers Farm, Chippenham, Wiltshire, SN14 6QA

Contents

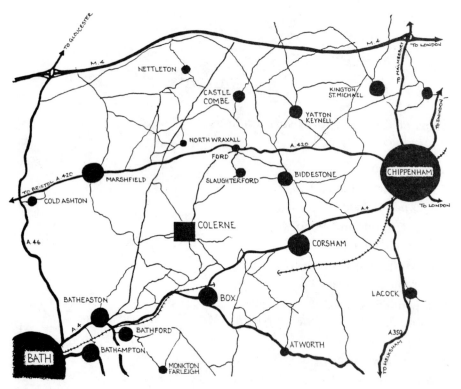

COLERNE
AND
SURROUNDING
AREAS

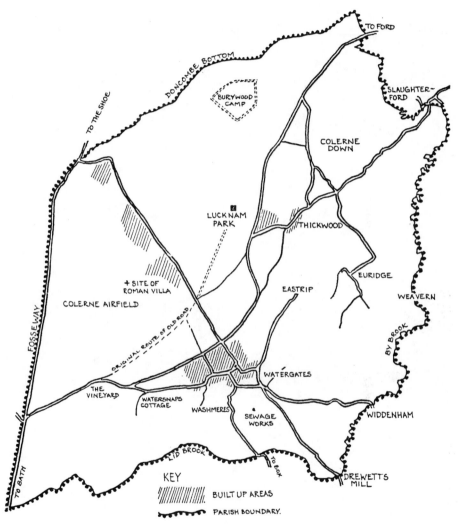

TO FORD

SLAUGHTER-
FORD

DONCOMBE BOTTOM

TO THE SHOE

BURYWOOD
CAMP

COLERNE
DOWN

LUCKNAM
PARK

THICKWOOD

+ SITE OF
ROMAN VILLA

EURIDGE

COLERNE AIRFIELD

EASTRIP

WEAVERN

FOSSEWAY

ORIGINAL ROUTE OF OLD ROAD

BY BROOK

WATERGATES

THE
VINEYARD

WATERSNAPS
COTTAGE

WASHMERES

SEWAGE
WORKS

WIDDENHAM

LID BROOK

TO BOX

TO BATH

DREWETTS
MILL

KEY

//////// BUILT UP AREAS

•••••• PARISH BOUNDARY.

© Crown copyright.

Foreword

Our village name

The present spelling of the name of our village, Colerne, is the same as that used in Domesday Book (1086), but it appears only a little later as Culerna or Culerne in the Malmesbury Register of 1156, and there seems to have been persistent alternation between the two spellings (sometimes as Collerne or Cullerne) right up to the last century. The local pronunciation of the name clearly relates to the *cul* form.

In "The Place-names of Wiltshire" by Gover, Mawer and Stenton (1939) it is suggested that this early alternation makes the name difficult to interpret. They say "The second element is clearly *aern*, 'house'. *col-aern* might well denote a house where charcoal was made, used or stored" and quote another source which attributes the same meaning to *cul*.

Other writers have suggested different meanings. In his "Notes on Wiltshire Names", John C. Langstaff (1911) says "the situation of the village lends some support to the suggested derivation of the first syllable from Welsh or Cornish *col*, a peak. Hence the 'dwelling on the peak'. It may, however, be 'the cold dwelling' from AS [Anglo-Saxon] *cald*, cold". He also suggests a possible derivation from the surname, Cole, of a Wiltshire landowner. More recently, in "Wiltshire Place Names", Richard Tomkins (1983) seems to have been influenced by the *cul* spelling in suggesting "the household of Cula", but he, too, recognises that "as Colerne stands on the hillside above the steep coombe formed by the By Brook, the first element may be derived from the Welsh word *col*, descriptive of a peak or summit".

In naming this book, we have been influenced not only by that suggested derivation, but also by the many generations of travellers between Bath and London, on what is now the A4, who have looked across the valley from Box Hill, seen our church on the skyline and wondered about that "village on the hill".

Population

As Stephen Whyte's chapter points out, Colerne has been a place of settlement for human beings since at least the Iron Age; and it has been quite an important place for much of that time. It is obviously difficult to estimate populations for very early times, but there may well have been as many as 500 people associated with Bury Wood Camp, and a similar number would seem appropriate for the Romano-British settlements in our area. The population may have declined somewhat in the Anglo-Saxon period, in common with the country generally, but Colerne was still relatively important at the time of Domesday Book (1086) and in the Middle Ages.

From then on, there was probably a very slow, but steady, growth up to the time of the first census in 1801 when the Colerne population was put at 693; at this time there were a little over 180,000 inhabitants in Wiltshire and only 9.2 million in the whole of England and Wales. During the next forty years Colerne expanded rapidly to 1209 in 1841; but this included 66 labourers on the construction of the Great Western Railway (and some of their families) and by 1851 the total was back to 1086.

Colerne's population then stayed very stable for the rest of the nineteenth century, but after 1901 there was a fairly rapid decline to 844 in 1931. The coming of the RAF in 1939 changed all that. In 1951 – the first census after the war – the population was 2035 and it rose to a peak of 3142 in 1971. The withdrawal of the RAF and its replacement by the Army led to a reduction to 2221 in 1981, but since then there has been new development and the estimated population in 1989 was 2483.

Over the last 190 years Colerne has grown, declined and then grown again to almost three-and-a-half times its 1801 population. The population of Wiltshire, which remains a mainly rural county, has increased by a slightly smaller proportion, while the population of England and Wales as a whole is more than five times its 1801 total. But, looking back much further, Colerne probably now has five to ten times its population in the Iron Age, whereas that of England and Wales has increased a hundred-fold.

A note on money

Most of the contributions in this book relate to the period before 1971, so amounts of money are expressed in pounds (£), shillings (s) and pence (d). There were, of course, twelve pence in a shilling and twenty shillings in a pound. A penny could be divided into halves and quarters, called halfpennies and farthings.

We have tried to be consistent in the way we have written amounts of money. Our standard form is like this: £4 14s 7d. We have used this form even in quotations where the original document may have expressed it differently (e.g. 10/- for 10s 0d).

Of course, the value of money has changed a great deal over the years, particularly since the end of the 1939–45 war. Some idea of what it would buy in the early nineteenth century can be obtained from the list on page 109; it is also worth noting that the normal agricultural wage at that time was about 10s 0d a week, or less.

J. U.

Acknowledgements

Colerne History Group would like to thank all the many people who have helped to make this book possible. Joyce Utting has been the prime mover in achieving the History Group's objective of producing this book on time. In addition to her contributions to two chapters, she has enthused the whole group with her persuasive pressure to meet deadlines, and has co-ordinated all the final stages of production.

John Chandler, then Local Studies Officer for Wiltshire, and Clare Higgens, of Box, gave valuable help and advice in the very early days; the local history groups at Wroughton and Atworth encouraged us by their example; Colerne Parish Council has lent an office and the Wiltshire Rural Initiatives Fund helped to equip it; the staff at the Wiltshire Record Office and Local Studies Library have been unfailingly helpful in pointing the way to material and helping us to find our way through it, and so has the Archivist of New College, Oxford; Joan and Arthur Platt have allowed us to have most of our meetings in the historical setting of Daubeneys; a number of people have given typing and secretarial assistance, Alison Maitland and David Utting have lent us their word processor, and we have had willing access to Colerne Primary School's photo-copier.

"A History of Colerne", published by Colerne Women's Institute some years ago, has provided useful background reading for several of our authors. Its coverage is much wider than that of the present volume which does not attempt to be a replacement for it.

Many members of our group and other village residents who are not authors of chapters have contributed valuable information; among them, mention should be made of Arthur Platt and Margaret Wood whose researches have dug out material which has been used by several of our authors. We should also mention those older villagers who have allowed us to interview them about Colerne life earlier in this century. Some of their memories have been used in this book, but most of them have been reserved for a booklet on 'growing up in Colerne' which we hope to publish in October 1990.

Printing arrangements have been handled by Donald Thompson, who has provided all typesetting facilities. His invaluable experience of all aspects of getting into print has guided us in our pursuit of editorial and typographic excellence.

We have been greatly helped in financing this publication by all those who have assisted or supported our various fund-raising activities, and particularly by the many people who have helped to provide money 'up front' by ordering their copies in advance of publication.

Illustrations

The maps on pp vi and vii were designed by Brian Vowles and are reproduced by permission of the Ordnance Survey. The drawing on p 14 is by William Knight and those on pp 18 and 24 are by Roger Clifton. Adrian Wood has provided the maps and illustrations for his own chapter and some other photographs. All the photographs of memorials and a number of others were taken by Dennis Coles. We are grateful to all those people who have made other photographs and illustrations available to us. We have endeavoured to obtain permission to reproduce any to which copyright may apply, and we offer our apologies to any copyright owners we may have overlooked or failed to trace.

R. G. C.

Introduction

Everyone likes to feel that there is something special about the place they live in. It has got to be prettier, or more interesting, or happier, or less spoilt, than its neighbours. So what makes Colerne special?

To find the beginnings of an answer, stand at night time by the main road out of Box. Look northwards, and you will see a cluster of lights high on the hilltop. That is Colerne, surrounded by darkness and standing aloof on the very last edge of the Cotswolds. It is an isolated spot, in spite of its nearness to Bath and Chippenham.

This isolation has helped to shape Colerne's character over the centuries. During the Iron Age, people liked its lonely and commanding position and built a hillfort here. The Romans constructed a villa nearby, close to the Fosse Way. Through the Middle Ages and beyond, Colerne blossomed into a busy and prosperous settlement. Yet it remained remote. When winter storms swept over from the east and blocked the lanes, it became cut off in a world of its own. Even today, blizzards and hurricanes can make it inaccessible for a few hours.

Because of this, Colerne has developed differently from most other villages near Bath. On the one hand, it has lagged behind them. Modern services, such as buses, sewerage, running water and doctors, came here late. On the other hand, it has kept a stable community where many inhabitants can still claim connection with long-established village families. Stability has also encouraged a kind of stubborn independence, which can clearly be seen in the wide variety of non-conformist churches.

Colerne's history has been a long and intriguing one. This book is the first concerted attempt to make something of it. It will not, by any means, be the last. Even while the book was being researched and written, members were eagerly jotting down ideas for a second volume. What, for example, of the Great Fire of Colerne? Did the ancient game of stowball, once played on Colerne Down, have any connection with golf? Why was the village renowned for its beer in the eighteenth century? And who was William Grocyn? Find out in our next absorbing instalment.

A. L.
February, 1990

Colerne: a Wiltshire Village

Stephen Whyte

Colerne is an attractive site for settlement. Situated on an abutting spur of the great oolite (limestone) ridge (about 540 feet above sea level) it dominates the surrounding landscape. The sparse woodland cover on the plateau (Sewell Wood and Colerne Park) means that the site is exposed to the southerly and north-easterly winds, and in winter it can be very cold. There is a good supply of water, with several springs rising in the area – the Market Place, Watergates and Tutton Hill.

The soil consists of pale limestone fragments, dry and not very fertile. This produces grasses admirably suited to the feeding of dairy cattle. Lower down the escarpment the development of loamy soils on superficial deposits of oolite gravels has favoured the cultivation of cereal crops.

The village lies mid way between Bath and Chippenham, about seven miles from each.

The Later Stone Age (c6000–2500 BC)

The earliest evidence for settlement in Colerne is marked by the Three Shire Stones, on the western boundary of the parish. The present stones are not original, but were erected in the Victorian era, superseding three smaller stones which were allowed to remain undisturbed beneath the central slabs.

The Shire Stones are recorded as a burial chamber on the Ordnance Survey map of neolithic Wessex, but not by Dr Glyn Daniel in his book "The Prehistoric Tombs of England and Wales". The stone tools found in the area consist of a core and blade of microlithic type,[1]

---

[1] A 'core' is a lump of flint from which flakes or blades have been struck; 'microlithic' indicates that they are of very small flints.

1

common in the Middle Stone Age, and a core, flint scrapers and flint axe of later origin.

The hunter gatherers who passed through Colerne may have erected temporary wooden shelters, but the evidence for the former existence of these structures has been destroyed by nature or man.

The Bronze Age (c2400–700 BC)

Wessex is notable for its Bronze Age sites, but the evidence for any settlement in Colerne at this time is, at best, uncertain. It consists of a group of three circular mounds, one large, with a surrounding ditch, in Colerne Park. The summit of the largest mound was flat, with a diameter of 25 ft. The Bronze Age round barrow or mound contained the remains of a single burial. Only excavation will determine whether these are burial mounds but the large quantities of building stone and roofing tiles suggest that they may have been Romano-British rubbish heaps. The only bronze object found in the area was a flat bronze or copper axe.

The mounds must be established as Bronze Age barrow burials before we can postulate the existence of some form of permanent settlement.

The Iron Age (c600 BC–45 AD)

The promontory hillfort on Northwood Plain was the first large and permanent form of settlement at Colerne. The excavations of D Grant-King in the 1960s clearly established that Bury Wood Camp was one of the later and more developed types of hillfort.

The fort was defended on the south by two rows of banks and ditches, approached from the level plateau; and on the north and east by one bank, protected by steep natural scarps. The banks were originally nine to ten feet high with a dump construction of earth and small stones behind.

The interior of the hillfort is about 32 acres in area. There were three entrances, on the south, the north-west and the north-east. All of these entrances overlapped, but the most interesting was the north-east. Here a tunnel-shaped passageway led into the interior through a huge timber gate tower. The sides of the passageway were constructed of vertical dry stone walling. The main finds consisted of pottery, some coinage and animal bones.

The pottery was of the plain coarse type without any trace of decoration (saucepan pots and buckets), and is difficult to date, but the Iron Age coinage is more helpful and suggests a date of around 100 BC.

Bury Wood Camp was inhabited by one of the Celtic tribes of the south-west, the Dobunni or the Belgae, whose economy was based on agriculture. Although there is no evidence of the cultivation of cereals, there is evidence of the existence of large numbers of domesticated animals, such as sheep, oxen, pigs and poultry.

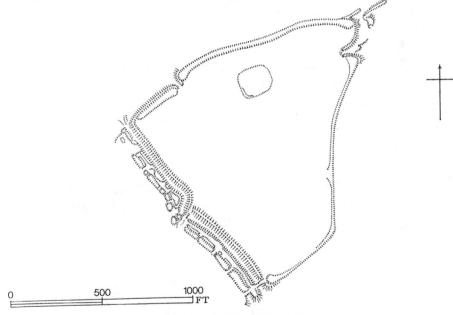

Fig 1   Ground plan of Bury Wood Camp

Barry Cunliffe has suggested in his book "Iron Age Communities in Britain" that the later hillforts were early towns whose economies were based on agriculture and industry.

We know that agriculture played an important part in the life of the community at Bury Wood, but until the interior of the hillfort is excavated, we can only speculate that industry here was comparable

with that at Danebury in Hampshire, which is believed to have had a
population of some 500 to 1000.

The Romans

The Romans quickly conquered the south-west. Bury Wood Camp
may have been attacked by the second Augustan legion on its march to
Gloucester, as it commanded the route west via the Chippenham Gap.
To secure their control of the countryside the Romans built roads, and
the Fosse Way forms the first frontier in the west, as well as serving as
an important military way. The development of Bath as a spa with the
baths and temple complex at its centre, and access via the Fosse Way,
facilitated the romanisation of the Colerne area and the building of
villas.

There is good evidence for the Roman development of Colerne with
several possible Roman sites having been identified in the area. The
best-known is the villa near the runway on the RAF station (now the
Azimghur Barracks), which was excavated by E Godwin in 1854. The
stone and timber building began as an aisled structure but was later
modified into a house with an attached suite of baths. The building
consisted of eleven rooms, three tessellated pavements and a hypo-
caust. The best of the pavements depicted a chariot with a charioteer
and four horses abreast, above which was the inscription "Servis" or
"Severus". Two stone coffins containing the complete skeletons of
small children were also found near the site of this villa.

The classic definition of the Roman villa is that given by R G
Collingwood in "The Archaeology of Roman Britain":

> Villa in Latin means farm. It is an economic term and refers to the fact that
> the place so designated is an agricultural establishment. There is a popular
> tendency to restrict its application to the country houses of the rich with
> luxury accessories and an ambitious plan, but there is no good reason for
> any such restriction. Any house of the Roman period may be called a Villa,
> provided it was the dwelling of people somewhat romanised in manners,
> who farmed a plot of land, as opposed to a town house on the one hand and
> a cottage on the other.

The villa at Colerne suggests that the owner or tenant possessed some
degree of wealth. If so, then he may well have invested some of the

surplus profit from agriculture in the stone industry. The Romans had the technology to exploit the local beds of oolitic limestone (Innox, Sewell Wood and Widdenham) and free stone was probably quarried in the area.

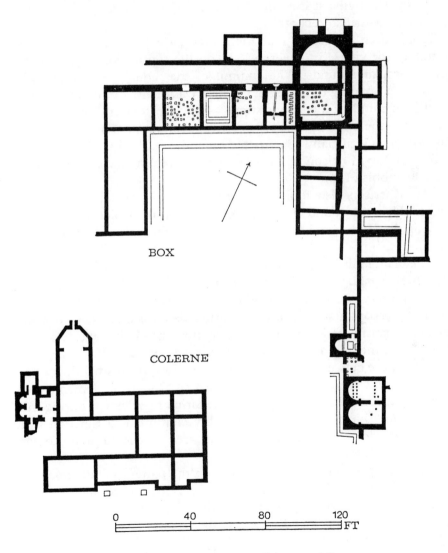

Fig 2   Plans of Roman villas at Colerne and Box

It is possible that the villa at Colerne was part of a larger agricultural estate, with its centre at Box, where there is a large Courtyard Villa. Colerne is one of several known villas within a two and a half mile radius of Box. If the estate owner, a Roman or his bailiff, lived in the more splendid villa at Box, then the outlying villas were probably run by Romano-British tenants.

It has been suggested that there may have been another Roman building (or villa?) in Colerne Park on the top of the largest of the three circular mounds. The summit of the mound was sufficiently large for a building of some kind. There was plenty of building debris in the surrounding ditch consisting of building stone and roofing tiles. However, the building of a villa or any other substantial structure on the top of an artificially constructed mound is most unlikely, so we are left with Mr Morrison's interpretation of the mound, as a Romano-British rubbish heap.

Mr Morrison also found evidence for a Roman site at Euridge Farm. Here he found a fragment of sculpture depicting Hercules slaying the Hydra, and a scatter of pottery, coins and tiles over a wide area.

The main finds from these sites are building debris, including stone, flue tiles, roofing slabs, copper nails, glass, wall plaster, tessellated floors, pottery and coins. The glossy, highly-decorated pottery and a coin of Vespasian suggest a first century date for settlement but the greater quantity of fourth and fifth century material suggests a later date. If so, then we are confronted with a gap of about three hundred years or more between the capture of the hillfort, the dismantling of its defences, and the establishment of the first Roman settlements. We can only speculate about changes in the form of settlement during this period, but Bury Wood Camp probably continued to function as a focal point for the inhabitants of the area. Some limited Roman settlement may have taken place.

It is thus possible to detect changes in the pattern of settlement at Colerne during the Iron Age and Roman period – when there appears to have been a movement away from the larger and more centralised location (as at Bury Wood) towards the smaller and more scattered type of settlement (the villa).

The Saxons

There is evidence of some form of Saxon settlement at Colerne. The name 'Colerne' may itself be derived from two Anglo-Saxon name elements – 'Col' meaning 'cold' and 'erne' meaning 'a dwelling'. A cold dwelling would certainly have been an apt description of Colerne during a bad winter!

The Anglo-Saxon chronicle records Saxon victories at Old Sarum (552 AD), Barbury Castle (556) and Dyrham (557), as Wiltshire came under West Saxon control. Later the fortified town of Chippenham was captured by the Danes (Vikings) in 875, in their attempt to conquer the Saxon kingdom of Wessex.

Two stone fragments from the cross head of a Saxon cross, perhaps erected to mark one stage in the journey of St Aldhelm from Doulting to Malmesbury (in 804 AD) can be found in the church of St John the Baptist.

The two stone fragments are rough irregular slabs, with only one face; both are covered with fine dragonesque sculpture, in which the bodies of the beasts are ornamented with various conventional patterns. Pevsner's "Wiltshire" suggests that they date from the ninth century, which is consistent with the Aldhelm connection. The existing 'Saxon' cross in the churchyard is a reproduction and was designed by the late Sir Harold Brakespear of Box.

There is a large gap in our knowledge relating to settlement at Colerne during the Saxon period, which is largely due to the failure to find any Saxon dwellings in the area. Though we might not expect to find much structural evidence for settlement in the pagan Saxon period (up to 700 AD) there was certainly a well established settlement at Colerne before the Domesday Book was compiled in 1086. This lists the names of several Saxon owners of land in Colerne before 1066, who subsequently lost their estates to Normans. Leofnoth held Colerne, and Swein similarly held Thickwood prior to 1066.

There were ninth century Saxon settlements at Corsham and Chippenham.

If it could be established that the existing Norman church had a Saxon predecessor, then we would be able to locate the centre of the

Saxon settlement. The form of that settlement would, however, still remain a problem for further investigation.

The Normans

After the conquest, Colerne was granted to Humphrey of the Island, or de Lisle, one of the companions of William the Conqueror, who held the Barony of Castle Combe, which included Colerne and twenty-six other villas or manors in Wiltshire. In Domesday Book Colerne was described as follows:

> Leofnoth held it before 1066; it paid tax for 10 hides, land for twelve ploughs, of which four and a half hides are in Lordship;
> 3 ploughs there; 10 slaves; 13 villagers and 5 cottagers with 8 ploughs.
> A mill which pays 13s 6d; meadow, 8 acres; a small wood one league long and another wide. The value was and is £10.

So by 1086 Colerne was a large manor, with the manor house and the wooden dwellings of the 13 villagers and 5 cottagers at the centre of the estate, surrounded by 1200 acres of land under cultivation, 1440 acres of woodland and 8 acres of meadow. The manor also possessed one mill (Widdenham). There were eleven ploughs in use suggesting a total of at least 88 oxen on the manor.

Domesday Book also mentions Thickwood, Lucknam and Euridge, all of which are now in the parish of Colerne. The most important of these was the hamlet of Thickwood, which was granted at the Conquest to Edward of Salisbury. In Domesday Book Thickwood is described as follows:

> Swein held it before 1066; it paid tax for 2 hides. Land for 2 and a half ploughs, 2 ploughs in Lordship with 6 cottagers. Meadow, 3 acres; pasture as many. The value was 30s; now 40s.

The fact that the hamlet at Thickwood was a smaller settlement than the manor at Colerne is supported by the lower acreage under cultivation (240 acres) and the smaller population of the estate.

The ownership and the extent of the settlements or estates at Lucknam (Lucas Hamlet) and Euridge (Yew Tree Ridge) are not given in Domesday Book, but a Ewrugge (presumably Euridge) was granted to Malmesbury Abbey by King Athelstan.

So according to Domesday Book there was a large manor at Colerne, two smaller hamlets, at Thickwood and Lucknam, and one or two buildings at Euridge. The pattern of settlement within the parish was therefore scattered over a wide area, although the actual village of Colerne was probably already beginning to take on the appearance of a nucleated settlement.

The Medieval period

The main source of information for Colerne during the Medieval period (from about 1200 to 1600) comes from a wide variety of documentary sources, of which the Malmesbury Register, the manorial rolls and the tax returns are some of the more important. These sources reveal something of the social and economic changes which the village experienced during this period.

We can trace the history of the village so well during these centuries because for much of the period it was the property of Malmesbury Abbey or of the Warden and Scholars of New College, Oxford, both of which kept meticulous records of their property in Colerne.

The Manor house and the church were the focal points of village life during the Middle Ages, and by tracing the history of these buildings we can see something of the process of change in the village.

The Manor

As we have seen, the Manor of Colerne was granted to Humphrey de Lisle, following the Norman conquest. Later it passed into the hands of the first baron of Castle Combe, Walter de Dunstanville, and after the third baron's death in 1270 to Sir John Delamere. He had a subtenant, Sir Geoffrey de Wroxhale, from whom, we know, Robert le Seneschal also held "land and tenements" in Colerne; so it appears that the original estate was already being broken up into smaller units.

On 30th November 1274, in a deed which can be found in the Malmesbury Register, Sir Geoffrey de Wroxhale confirmed a gift of lands and tenements in Colerne, which had been made by Robert le Seneschal to the Abbot (William of Colerne) and Convent of St Aldhelm at Malmesbury. In return, Sir Geoffrey was to receive an annual rent of five pence and aid whenever the national taxes of scutage and hideage were levied.

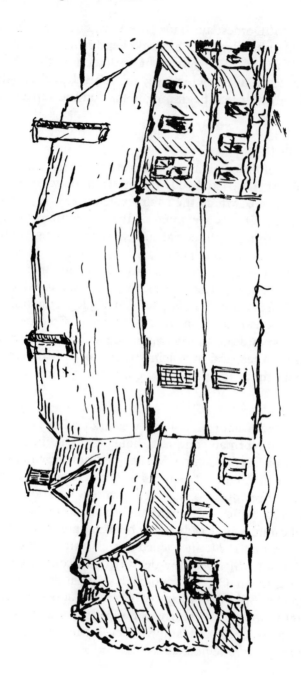

COLERNE MANOR HOUSE.
N.E. VIEW.

Fig 3   Drawing of Manor House, c1900

This estate was distinct from the Manor, which passed through a variety of hands during the next hundred years. In 1388 the reversion was sold to William of Wykeham (who founded both Winchester College and New College, Oxford) by Elizabeth, the daughter of Bartholomew de Burghesh and wife of Edward le Despenser, for 700 marks (about £450), and he conveyed it to New College in the following year. This property consisted of the Manor and demesne (the lord's own lands) and was separated from the rest of the village. New College did not sell the Manor until 1877.

The great hall of the Manor was where the lord (or his steward) showed hospitality, administered justice, appointed his local officials their tasks and received his dues. He was entitled to various other payments from his tenants in addition to their rents. These included 'tallage', a tax which was levied prior to 1400, payments for pasturage of cattle and pigs on his lands and woods, called 'herbage' and 'pannage', and 'Lord's silver' which was a payment instead of former gifts in kind for his table, and which was commonly charged at 1d or 2d a head.

The Manor court was held twice a year at Martinmas (11th November) and at Hockeday, a feast which was held on the second Monday and Tuesday after Easter to celebrate the liberation of England from the Danes. We know that at one of these courts, in 1441, Agnes Boteler was to be seized for house-breaking and stealing two goblets and 4d from Alice Gregory. At another court (the 'View of Frankpledge' which dealt with minor offences) on 20th June 1405, Maud, wife of John Mallman, was presented as "a common scold and disturber of the peace" and was to be punished by a ducking. Her husband paid 4d to relax this judgement.

The granting of a fair or market was a mark of favour by the King in return for services in war. A charter to hold a market carried with it the right to levy market tolls which often made another useful contribution to the Lord's income. In 1447 Henry VI granted to the Warden and Scholars of New College a market at Colerne every Friday and a fair for three days on the vigil, day and morrow of the beheading of St John the Baptist (28–30th August).

The Parish Church

The oldest part of the church (the eastern end of the present nave) was built by Walter de Dunstanville between 1190 and 1195, and the chancel by the third baron of Castle Combe who bore the same name. The chapel, north aisle and clerestory to the nave were added in 1280 probably under the direction of William of Colerne. Later additions were made under the auspices of New College, the tower dating from about 1450.

The list of known rectors and vicars dates from 1298; the church registers go back to 1560; and the churchwardens' account books start from 1692.

The church enjoyed the patronage of the lords of Colerne. They may have contributed to the upkeep and maintenance of the church for genuine spiritual reasons, but their generosity could, in part, also have been motivated by the fact that the market was often held in the churchyard. They would therefore have needed to maintain the goodwill of the rector or curate, so as to ensure the use of the churchyard and the nave of the church on market day.

The Medieval village

There are three other buildings in the village which certainly have a foundation date before 1600, Daubeneys and numbers 1 and 3 Market Place, and there are medieval features in others; but it is difficult to estimate the full extent of the village in that period.

Daubeneys, now a private dwelling-house, is an excellent example of a medieval longhouse, a type of farmhouse in which the farmer and his stock were housed under one roof, so as to give easy access to the stock. It belonged to the Abbey of Malmesbury as tenant of the Manor, and the house may have been built by William of Colerne. One of the properties he acquired in the village has already been mentioned: the copyhold given to the Abbey by Robert le Seneschal in 1274. (A copyhold was a long-term tenure, the ownership of which could be proved by referring to the 'copy' in the manorial records; it was the usual means of paying a steward, who received the profit or rent from the copyhold in return for his services.) It has been suggested that this copyhold may have been identical with Daubeneys,

Fig 4   Fragment of Saxon cross and Medieval figure of a saint set in north wall of parish church

which was described as a copyhold in the possession of Mary and Ann Drewett in 1787. The upper floor was probably added about 1390 by New College shortly after the College acquired the Manor of Colerne.

Fig 5   Eastern end of Daubeneys

Numbers 1 and 3 Market Place are more modest buildings, a pair of one and a half storey rubble stone cottages which still have their stone-tiled roofs. They were probably occupied by freeholders, copyholders or tenants-at-will who derived their living from working the land or quarrying the free stone in the area.

The records show that there was further fragmentation of estates in the village after the end of the fourteenth century, as both secular and religious institutions and individuals acquired property there. By the time of the first Colerne Enclosure Award in 1787 the leading land-owners included New College, the governors of Charter House, Wentworth Parsons and Paul Methuen; and later, in 1873, a plan of New College properties in the village shows that they then owned about twenty, including the Manor House, Daubeneys and number 3 Tutton Hill, then two separate dwellings. However, a thorough search of the records – especially those relating to the properties of New College and Charter House – would be required to estimate the number of properties existing in Colerne in the medieval period.

A prosperous village

The growing wealth of the village in the Middle Ages suggests that there would have been money available to invest in property. This wealth is reflected in two fourteenth century tax assessments: the 'fifteenths and tenths' of 1334 and the 'Poll Tax' of 1377.

The assessment known as 'fifteenths and tenths' was based on a valuation of certain personal property, usually described by the vague word "moveables". Of this value, the King took a fraction which varied from grant to grant; but in each grant a greater proportion was levied on cities, towns and royal demesnes than on other areas. Thus in 1334 the townsman found himself contributing a tenth of his assessed moveables but the countryman only a fifteenth.

The range of the tax quotas in the hundred of Chippenham was large. At the top of the scale was Bremhill assessed at 310 shillings; at the foot were several tiny fiscal units assessed at twenty shillings or less. Colerne's assessment was 100 shillings; only Bremhill, Corsham, Kington St Michael, Lacock and Nettleton had a higher valuation.

There were several poll taxes in the fourteenth century, some of them widely evaded. That of 1337 was a flat rate of 4d a head (poll) levied on everyone over the age of fourteen who was not a professional beggar. There is a considerable variation in the number of tax payers in the different fiscal areas in the hundred of Chippenham. At the top

was Lacock with 355 taxpayers and at the bottom the Vill of Cockle-
bury where the collectors recorded only ten taxpayers. Colerne was
assessed at 168, and only ten per cent of all the places in Wiltshire had
as many.

These figures reveal that Colerne was one of the more prosperous
villages in the Chippenham area. The development of agriculture and
industry, on which this prosperity was based, is discussed further in
Adrian Wood's chapter of this book.

References

Blathwayt W E (1901), "The Manor House, Colerne" in the *Bath Natural
    History and Antiquarian Field Club Proceedings*, vol 9, pp 150–158, Bath.
Crittall E and Pugh R B (eds) (1973), *The Victoria County History of
    Wiltshire* vols 1–5, O.U.P., Oxford.
Cunliffe B (1974), *Iron Age Communities in Britain* (2nd edn.), Routledge and
    Kegan Paul, London.
Daniel G (1950), *The Prehistoric Chamber Tombs of England and Wales*,
    C.U.P., Cambridge.
Godwin E and Heathcote G (1856), "The Roman Villa at Colerne" in the
    Archaeological Journal, vol 13, pp 325–332, London.
Godwin E (1857), "An account of the church of St. John the Baptist,
    Colerne" in the *Wiltshire Archaeological and Natural History Magazine*,
    vol 3, pp 358–66, Devizes.
Grant-King D (1963), "Bury Wood Camp" in the *Wiltshire Archaeological
    and Natural History Magazine*, vol 58, pp 40–47, Devizes.
Thorne C F (1979), *Domesday Book. 6. Wiltshire*, Phillimore & Co. Ltd.,
    Chichester.

Parish Church and People 1750–1900

Roger Clifton

As it was the octocentenary of the parish church which provided the impetus for this book, it seemed natural to ask the rector to provide an article on the church; but with eight hundred years to choose from, where does one start? There is already a leaflet containing the history of the building – so it seemed a good idea to dip into the registers. When we look through the faded pages of baptisms, marriages and burials, and the carefully written records of meetings long past, we see in front of us the life which has gone on for centuries in our village.

Although Colerne parish church is a very ancient foundation, it does not have a great many old records. In common with most other parishes, the Colerne records are now held by the Wiltshire County Records Office in Trowbridge. Conditions there are far healthier for old documents than a damp vestry, and public access is in many ways simpler.

The purpose of this chapter is only to give a feel of church and village life in the past from the records that we have, and the best source for this is the churchwardens' account book for the years 1755 to 1868. It is the oldest book we possess, and is beautifully written. The care in the handwriting is not matched, however, by the spelling, which varies wildly! (We have copied the original spellings here.) The church-wardens were (and still are) the "proper guardians and keepers of the parish church", and were required to present annual accounts to the vestry meeting. Vestry meetings go back over 600 years, and in the past performed many of the functions that are now the responsibility of local government. The administration of church affairs and village affairs were closely intertwined, and the wardens had wide ranging responsibilities.

The overall impression when looking through this account book is

RGC 1990

Fig 6   Parish church of St John the Baptist

one of uneventful continuity. The same names and expenses recur steadily, and very rarely does the outside world seem to impinge on the village. Most remarkable to a modern reader is the total absence of inflation – the totals for each year are almost unchanged throughout the 113 years covered by the book. The accounts are made up to Lady Day (March 25) each year until 1791, when it changes to Easter Day. The accounting period nowadays is the calendar year.

What did they spend their money on? Repairs to the church were the largest expense:

1759:	Thos and John Sumsion for mending pinicles	£5 3s 0d
1772:	Bells rehung by Josiah Robins for	£20 0s 0d
	[this was only 35 years after the tenor bell had been recast and a sixth bell added. A further two were added at the restoration of 1877 to make the present peal of eight]	
1782:	Paid for beer for men repairing the church window	7d
	[this often appears for various jobs and appears to be in lieu of wages]	

In a slightly later account book we find:

1871:	Jas Butler for new seats.	£13 7s 4d
	Transport of new organ from Warminster, two wagons and six horses	£5 0s 0d

Repair works around the village were also dealt with:

1758:	John Mullins for pound geat	10s 0d
1781:	Pd Dan' Davis for pitching the footway in Vicarage Lane	£1 11s 6d

Vermin fees were another regular payment, for the benefit of the parish rather than the church. These were instituted by an Act of 1532, which was renewed regularly until the late nineteenth century. Vermin were caught, shown to the wardens and then destroyed. The scale of the payments suggests that it was a regular occupation for some people, though the names of the recipients are not given. Eight payments totalling 17s 0d were made in 1759 for foxes, and four totalling 4s 6d for rats. Vipers appear from 1803 onwards, and 238 were killed in 1823. We would not now regard some of the creatures as vermin, for example hedgehogs (1s 0d paid for six in 1800) or sparrows; no less than 139 dozen of these were destroyed in 1846, which seems slightly unbiblical.

The ordinary running expenses of the church were not large. "Violoncello strings" are a regular item, though we do not know when the traditional village church 'orchestra', employing the skills of several villagers, was replaced by the organ which needed only one person. Certainly there was an organist being paid £5 per annum in 1844. "Cleaning engine pipes" is another regular payment, because the fire engine was kept in the church. The ringers are paid for special occasions such as Wellington's funeral in 1852, and also have an annual treat: "5 Nov 1788, Paid the ringers feast, deducting 5s 0d for not ringing a ringing day, £1 6s 6d." Church cleaning was apparently done by the vestry clerk: "Apl 20 1824: At a vestry holden this day it was agreed that a salary of four guineas per year be given to the clerk – for which salary he is to do his duty in a proper manner, keep the church well cleaned and swept, and the clock regularly wound up." Sometimes, however, he needed help: "1822, Hannah Milsham for scouring the sconce – 5s 0d". There is no record of any heating in the church until 1839, when coal for the stove becomes a regular expense.

The account books give us glimpses of all sorts of other matters of which we would love to know more. For example, paying 1s 6d in 1821 for two bushels of lime for whitewashing the School Room – where was it? The National School first gets a mention in 1833, and the Sunday school in 1902. In July 1824 they paid "men for cleaning the new blind house with fire engine 2s 0d." The wardens paid £7 in 1813 for a "new iron chest" – where did that go? In 1815 it cost 10d to post a letter to Salisbury, about half a day's agricultural wage. In 1837 the expenses of the Guardians of the Poor appear for the first time. Before the changes in the Poor Law there were often payments to those who had been given a pass by a magistrate to seek alms: "4 Dec 1755: To a pas 4 disabled semen 6d." At this period there were regular routes along which sailors walked between ports to find work, and quite a few turn up with passes to receive alms from the parish.

These then were the regular expenses of the parish, typical of countless others in England. Where did they find the income to meet them? The main source of funds was for many centuries the church rate, which like other rates was a levy based on property. It developed

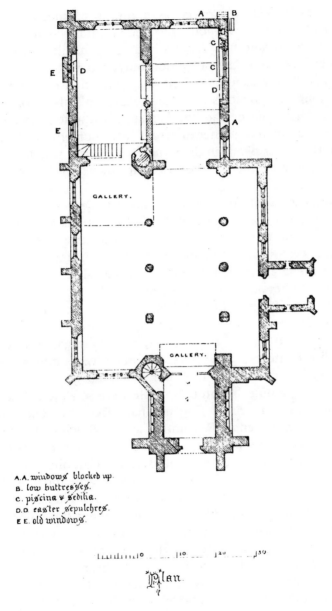

A.A. windows blocked up.
B. low buttresses.
c. piscina & sedilia.
D.D easter sepulchres.
E E. old windows.

Plan.

Fig 7   Plan of the parish church before restoration in 1877

in the mid-fourteenth century as a means of meeting occasional deficits in church accounts, but continued until it was abolished in the middle of the nineteenth century. It never had a statutory basis, remaining a common law obligation only, but was still compulsory. This was no doubt a source of irritation to the non-conformists of the parish (though the rector's reply to the Bishop's visitation queries of 1787 states that Colerne had "no Papists, no atheists, and one Quaker who is superannuated"; other dissenters are not mentioned). In 1774 a church rate of four pence in the pound was raised, which yielded £62 0s 6d and covered ninety per cent of the church expenditure for that year.

Following the abolition of church rates, we see churchgoers gradually waking up to their responsibilities. Collections start to appear in the accounts, but they also rely heavily on the generosity of the rector (one of the wealthiest people in the village according to the poor rate listings of the late eighteenth century) and local landowners. In 1891 the collections totalled £9 15s 5d, but the books were balanced by a donation of £8 from Squire Walmesley at Lucknam Park. It is interesting to see that over half the expenditure in that year was on wages of various kinds, to organist, verger, organ blowers, lamp lighters, fire lighters and cleaners. For many years now all such jobs (where they still exist) have been done voluntarily.

It is not surprising that churchpeople were so slow to change. For generations the Church of England had been the source of social stability. As the French Revolution of 1789 slipped into excess, English conservatism was stiffened, setting back such causes as the enfranchisement of dissenters and Roman Catholics. Church and State were considered to be one, and those who did not share the Anglican point of view were often treated badly. The church thought little about its doctrines and belief, and was largely immune to the new philosophical and theological movements in Germany and elsewhere. Worship too was dull and often carelessly performed. "People went to church on Sunday to learn to be good, to hear the commandments repeated to them for the thousandth time, and to see them written in gilt letters on the communion table" (J A Froude, 1886).

The problems came largely from above. Bishops were complacent and worldly, and the church was full of abuses which had existed from feudal times. During most of the period covered by our account books, the ministry was riddled with pluralism, absenteeism and gross inequality. A parson lived off his benefice, i.e. that from which he benefited. His 'living' had three main ingredients: glebe (land which had been given to the benefice by benefactors and which the parson farmed himself or let out), tithes (a percentage of the net profits of each landowner in his parish) and fees and offerings. The income of different parishes varied enormously, though 'Queen Anne's Bounty', established in 1704, gave some relief to the most needy benefices.

The man who received the income (the Rector) did not have to live in the parish, and in 1827, for example, three-fifths of the clergy were non-resident. They usually appointed a vicar or curate to care for the parish 'vicariously' in their absence, giving him some of the income (but not much). In 1830 the Bishop of Winchester earned £50,000 a year, while half the curates in the country earned less than sixty pounds. Despite all this, many struggling clergy carried on quiet and faithful lives of prayer and pastoral care in small parishes like Colerne, all over England, and gradually reform came about.

It was at first a spiritual reformation in the early years of the nineteenth century. The 'High Church' Oxford Movement led by clergy such as Keble and Newman, and the corresponding Evangelical Revival under men like Charles Simeon, created a new sense of holiness, a new zeal for mission and a rising social concern. Around this time we see the parish having collections towards the Royal United Hospital in Bath and making donations to missionary societies. The first of these, the SPCK and the SPG, were formed early in the eighteenth century, but the CMS, founded in 1799 by a group of evangelicals, was the first really effective one for mission abroad.

This spiritual awakening was followed by a wave of practical and legal reforms. In 1836 the Ecclesiastical Commissioners were established, to reform and redistribute church revenues. The Tithe Act of the same year commuted tithes, making them dependent on the varying price of corn. (Tithes became a fixed payment in 1918 and were gradually extinguished during the twentieth century. They now no longer exist.) Compulsory church rates were abolished. Poor glebe land was sold and the cash invested in government stock to give a better return for the benefice. Parliament did away with many of the abuses, and so by the mid-1800s clergy had far better conditions and a stable income, although there was still a lot of difference between 'poor' parishes and 'good' livings. It was not until the middle of this century that we reached the situation where all parochial clergy are now paid equally and the greater part of their income is provided by the people in the pew.

RGC 1990

Fig 8   Colerne rectory

This tide of revival led to all sorts of other changes. There were better and more inspirational bishops. The clergy were more awake to their duties and far more pastoral work was done, the church pioneering all kinds of social welfare which has gradually been assumed by the state. The Oxford Movement led (via much controversy) to fundamental improvements in the standard of worship. Rural deans and theological colleges were created to improve the organisation and the training of the clergy. Clubs and societies were founded, such as the Mothers Union and the Girls Friendly Society. The Convocations, which gave the membership some say in national church affairs, were re-established in 1854, not having met since 1717. Churches and parsonages were improved and many new ones built. The Church of England was in the forefront of educational reform too. School attendance was made compulsory for 5–10 year olds in 1882, and made free of charge in 1891, which led to a wave of schoolbuilding, most of it by the church.

All this was reflected in our own parish. In 1848 Gilbert Heathcote, the vicar at the time, gave the present Rectory to the church, as "the Parsonage House belonging to the said Vicarage of Colerne is inconvenient and too small and is not fit for the habitation of the Minister". (We do not, incidentally, seem to know where the previous parsonage was.) It is no wonder he found the old house too small – the census of 1861 showed the following people living in the (new) Rectory:

> Gilbert Heathcote, aged 44, Vicar
> Eliza Heathcote, 43, wife
> Mary Heathcote, 13, scholar
> Selina Heathcote, 11, scholar
> Frederick Heathcote, 9, scholar
> Ellen Heathcote, 7, scholar
> Elizabeth Davis, 25, governess
> Sarah Taylor, 38, housekeeper
> Hester Hillier, 19, children's maid
> Sarah Richards, 19, parlour maid
> Maria Gaisford, 16, housemaid.

No doubt there were also staff such as gardeners who were not resident. Mr Heathcote was a generous man and gave not only the Rectory, but much of the money for the school.

The reawakening of the church led to the well-known Victorian passion for 'restoring' church buildings, and Colerne was extensively rebuilt in 1877. The cost of nearly £4000 was met by Richard Walmesly of Lucknam Park, whose effigy lies in the south aisle, and Mr Poynder of Hartham Park near Corsham.

That is a good point at which to leave this brief look at some of the life of our parish and church. Many things have changed over the period covered by these old books of account; some we may regret, but most of them are changes for the better. Today's churchwardens may lead very different lives from their predecessors of 1755, and produce their accounts on a microcomputer instead of writing them in copperplate, but the Lord whom they serve, and the basic purpose of the church they care for, have not changed at all.

The Methodist Church in Colerne

Gordon Maynard

Origins

At the risk of appearing pretentious, to understand why there should have been a Methodist Church at Colerne, it is necessary to go back to events that started in England over 250 years ago.

Why Methodist? The name was a derisive term applied in 1729 to John Wesley, his brother Charles, George Whitfield and others – all members of the Anglican Church – because as graduates at Oxford University, they followed a severe moral discipline against a background of much dissipation and moral laxity, and because of their 'good works' amongst the poor and the prisoners in Oxford gaol. Being so rigid and methodical – they were called 'Methodists'.

John Wesley developed into a pious and rather prim high churchman. Despite his good works and self discipline, he felt that he "influenced no lives, touched no consciences, warmed no hearts". This is no place to describe his somewhat disastrous missionary efforts in the Colony of Georgia, but to come quickly to him as a dejected clergyman back in England, when, to use his own words, "I went unwillingly to a Moravian meeting at Aldersgate Street [London], on 24th May 1738 and heard one reading from Luther's preface to the Romans [possibly in Latin or German] and felt my heart strangely warmed – I felt I did trust in Christ". He was 35 years old.

John Wesley was so changed in his outlook that he tried to reform the Established Church by storm. He formed 'ginger groups', calling them "Methodist Societies". For the next 50 years he travelled 250,000 miles on horseback forming his Methodist Societies, insisting that the members took Communion in their parish churches. He tried to regard the societies as a "Connexion" rather than a denomination

27

Fig 9   Colerne Methodist chapel with its pre-war railings

and eschewed the term "dissenter". He averred that his intention
was to spread "Christian Holiness" throughout the land. But the
methodists were plainly a denomination, and after John Wesley had
appointed Thomas Coke as a bishop to work in America, the split was
inevitable.

After his death in 1791, the autocratic discipline was removed, there was occasional rebellion in the ranks, largely in matters of church government, not theology. Happily most of the dissenting parts were re-united at Westminster Central Hall in 1932 to form the Methodist Church.

The Primitive Methodist Church

The Primitive Methodist Church of which the Colerne Chapel was a part was the result of the efforts of Hugh Bourne (1772–1852) a Wesleyan Methodist, farmer and wheelwright in Tunstall in Staffordshire.

In 1807, he and some of his fellow preachers were seized with a desire to go into the byways, and onto convenient hill tops, and preach the Gospel to any who would hear. Thousands of poor ignorant folk listened.

The Methodist Church (Wesleyan) decided that it was no longer 'respectable' to do this. A 'Camp Meeting', as these gatherings were called, held on Mow Cop hill on 31 May 1807 from 6 am to 8 pm was the fuel, and Hugh Bourne's simple faith and unbounded enthusiasm was the spark, which led to the breach with the founder body. The Primitive Methodist Connexion was founded.

Hugh Bourne and his friends sent missions to central and northern England. They reached Brinkworth (near Wootton Bassett) in 1824. In 1832, the Revd J Barber was imprisoned at Chippenham for preaching in the Market Place. In 1835 the missionaries had formed a circuit of preaching places (mostly in rooms and outbuildings until their simple chapels could be built). Despite lack of money, and much opposition, chapels were built, often in the odd corners of fields. Religious faith and fervour coupled with a quite severe discipline earned the preachers the name "Ranters".

After six months they had eighteen places: at the end of the year they had 41. H Woodward was a preacher in charge at Thickwood in 1837.

County archives record the issue of a Meeting House Certificate in January 1836 for "A house and premises now in the holding of Henry Woodward of Thickwood". Until the last century the places where dissenters met for worship were supposed to be notified to the bishop, archdeacon or magistrates for the area, who issued a certificate. 'Certificates of Worship' are still issued for the Non-Conformist Churches.

In 1860 a small chapel was built at Thickwood opposite St Martins by local people. This was demolished in 1904. The Colerne 'Society' met in the old Club Room at the top of the yard at the Six Bells Inn.

Anniversary Celebrations – Thickwood

A Chapel Anniversary Tea Meeting organised at Thickwood on Wednesday 19th August 1902 for Colerne and Thickwood members, required the attendance of the Minister: Rev J Brayney, circuit steward C R Stevens, local preachers F W Woodward (Thickwood), George Maynard, H C Yeals (Colerne) and C Hancock (Box Hill). Such a meeting on a week day must have interfered with employment. The Anniversary culminated on the following Sunday with Mr C R Stevens as the preacher. Thickwood Chapel pews were the most uncomfortable ever designed! let us hope they were singing most of the time. This Anniversary must have been tinged with sadness because all would have been aware that the Chapel would close in the following October – but it may have been thought that the Colerne Chapel could cater for the needs of both communities.

Colerne

What were the marks of Primitive Methodism, and in particular Colerne Methodism: simple faith, unbounded hope and a desire to involve the working classes in the mission of the greater church universal. Apart from the centrality of the Bible and the exposition thereof, the sermon and singing were the distinguishing features. The hymns of Isaac Watts and Charles Wesley were the core, with hymns of all other branches of the church added to make the catholic whole. Every little chapel had a choir. In addition to the normal Christian festivals of Easter and Christmas, important events were the Chapel Anniversary, the Sunday School Anniversary and the Harvest Festival.

The Methodist Church
TICKET OF MEMBERSHIP

March 1969   O

'Thus says the Lord: Behold, what I have built I am breaking down, and what I have planted I am plucking up, that is the whole land. And do you seek great things for yourself?'

Jeremiah 45, 4, 5

Susan Maynard   LEP

A SHORT GUIDE TO THE DUTIES OF
CHURCH MEMBERSHIP

1. To come to Church every Sunday.
2. To join in Fellowship with other Christians in pursuit of a deeper experience of Christ.
3. To bear witness to Christ in daily life and to seek to win others.
4. To be methodical in prayer and Bible study.
5. To receive the Holy Communion faithfully and regularly.
6. To give personal service to Church, neighbours and community.
7. To give money for the work of the Church at home and overseas.

Fig 10 'Class Ticket'

Another distinctive feature of Methodism was the Class Meeting instituted by John Wesley. This was not only concerned with Bible Study and Moral Instruction but under its leader was responsible for the discipline of members. The Class Ticket was issued four times a year and was a sign of church membership and a precious thing to most. In former times it could be withheld from anyone who had fallen short in church attendances or was lax in general behaviour. Discipline was strict. In the middle of the last century, a youngish minister was hauled before the Quarterly Meeting and severely admonished for skating on a pond on the Sabbath!

PRIMITIVE METHODIST PREACHERS' PLAN.

CHIPPENHAM CIRCUIT, 1885.

"So they read in the book, in the Law of God, distinctly, and gave the sense, and caused them to understand the reading."—Neh. viii. 8.

"This is a faithful saying, and worthy of all acceptation, that Christ Jeus came into the world to save sinners."—*I. Timothy* i. 15.

Preachers' Names and Residences.

1 E. POWELL, Enfield Villa, Chippenham
2 J. BEST, St. Paul's Street, Chippenham
3 S. Hunt, Pickwick, Corsham
4 W. Cozens, Langley
5 G. Brittain, Studley
6 J. Little, Langley
7 G. Johnson. Derry Hill
8 G. Butler, New Road, Chippenham
9 G. Little, Langley
10 J. North, & H. Lowden
11 H. Baker, Colerne, *via* Box
12 G. Tavener, Slaughterford
13 L. Rumming, Langley   [ham
14 W. Moore, Westmead Lane, Chippen-
15 C. Hancock, Clare Cottage, Box Hill
16 C. R. Stevens, Market Place, Chippen-
17 J. E. Neate, Box Hill   [ham
18 J. Wicks, Butts, Chippenham
19 G. Elms, Wood Lane, Langley
20 J. Isaac, Colerne, *via* Box
21 E. Marsh, Market Place, Chippenham
22 J. Elliott, Langley
23 J. Lightfoot, St. Paul's St., Chippen-
24 M. Fishlock, Marshfield   [ham
25 T. Bull, Box
26 T. P. Cannings, Timber St., Chippen-
27 G. Maynard, Colerne, *via* Box   [ham
28 W. Bright, Colerne, *via* Box
29 F. Woodward, Thickwood, *via* Box
30 W. Hicks. Colerne, *via* Box
31 H. Mullins, Chippenham
32 E. Bowyer, London Rd.,Chippenham
33 G. Ponting, Cook Street, Chippenham
34 E. Beer. Derry Hill

35 W. Griffen, Biddestone

Exhorter.

36 F. B., Chippenham

Auxiliaries.

37 Rev. W. Newns, East Mead St., Calne
38 W. Bailey, Chittoe
39 J. Sansom, Bromham
40 A. Hinder. Poulshot
41 E. Ball, Steeple Ashton
42 E. Brown, Stockley
43 G. Drewett, Calne
44 H. Strange, Chittoe
45 J. Clemence, Caen Hill
46 S. Slade, Bremhill
47 F. March, Steeple Ashton
48 W. S. Tucker, Steeple Ashton

SOCIETY STEWARDS.	PLACES.	TIME.	OCTOBER				NOVEMBER					DECEMBER			
			4	11	18	25	1	8	)	22	29	6	13	20	27.
C. R. Stevens.	CHIPPENHAM	10½	1	18	10	50c	1	52c	1	1	RM	1	31 16	21	19c
	Monday	6	1	23	8	39c	19	52c	B	1s	RM	10	14	8	21c
		7¼	1	31	1	16	1	1	`	1	1	1	19	1	1
G. Cooper.	KINGTON) LANGLEY ...}	2½	9	36	8 c	8	4	21	1`	10c	6	22	13c	26	14
		6	9	18	Price	8	1 s	21	1!	10c	34	22	13c	26	14
	Tuesday	7	13			1		1:				1			1
H. Angell.	DERRY HILL	2½	8	21E	14	36	RM	40	1c	18	29	33	7	s s	22
	Wednesday	6	8s	21E	14	34	RM	40	1c	18	30	32	34	s s	22
		7	1			1	X		1:			1			1
S. Hunt.	CORSHAM	2½	25	19	34	RM	26	1c	8	24	13c	21	10	9	27c
	Tuesday	6	25	19	32	RM	26	1c	8	24	13c	21	10	9	27c
		7				1		1		1T		1			
E. Bence.	MARSHFIELD	2½	20	27	15c	51	25	29	R)	17	53c	28	1	24	51)
	Tuesday	5½	20	27	15c	51	25	29	R)	17	53c	28	1s	24`	51)
		7				1			1T			1Mon			
E. Tiley.	THICKWOOD	2½	15	CA	24	11	20c	12	9`	28	25c	30	27	s s	25
	Wednesday	6	15	CA	24	11	20c	12	^	28	25c	30	27	s s	25
J. North.	LOWDEN	2½	6	32	36	39	RM	10	9	13	1	10	8c	15	18
		6	6	31	26	50	RM	10	1	13	1s	31	8c	15	19
	Thursday	7¼	1	10	*	1	X	10	)	*	10	1	*	10	1
J. Skuse and W. Griffen.	BIDDESTONE	2½	12	6	24	14	RM	19	s	21	35	21	30	20	17
		6	12	6	24	14	RM	19	s	21	35	1c	30	20	17
	Thursday	7			1 s			1T			1				
C. Hancock.	BOX HILL	3	17	28	30c	54	27	RM	)	25	55	57c	29	10	1
		6	17	28	30c	54	27	RM	)	25	55	57c	29	10	1s
	Thursday	7	25	1	1T	15	1	25	1T	1r	15	25	1	17	15
H. Baker.	COLERNE	2½	11		1	28	17	24	3	27	51	25	15		30
	Wednesday	6	11		1s	28	17	24	3	27	51	25	15		30
		7	1 Tues	1	28	11	1T	30	3	11	28	27	1	30	27
G. Tavener.	SLAUGHTER-FORD.........	2½	26	22	35	s s	28	33	D	9	57c	1`	19	13c	11
		6	26	22	35	s s	28	32	D	9	57c	1`	19	13c	11

Fig 11   Part of a preaching list

Town churches might be 'pseudo-gothic', but the minister must be soberly dressed and liturgical services would not be much in evidence. The minister would officiate at the services of Holy Communion: otherwise the pulpit was occupied by the 'local preacher'. He would have to take examinations in theology and the art of preaching, but he was drawn from the ranks of farmers, labourers, artisans and shop keepers. A preacher who failed to keep his appointments was 'dropped a place' on the 'Preaching List'. Up to the 1920s most would be expected to walk up to fifteen miles in all weathers to take one or two appointments on a Sunday. The better-off might share a pony and trap.

Space allows but one account of an individual preacher. From a treasured note-book owned by Mrs Joyce Hulbert, we have a record of sermon subjects taken by her grandfather, Mr Walter Hicks, in the Methodist chapels (and Congregational chapels) in this area. On the extract of the Plan of 1885 he is Number 30, in 1896 he is at Number 18.

The Camp Meeting, referred to earlier, was still a feature of Primitive Methodism up to the turn of the century. The Quarterly Meeting at Chippenham on 11th March 1867 decided that "open air services be held at Colerne and that Camp Meetings be held at Thickwood". Records are hazy but it seems that they were held in a convenient field, lasted most of the day and ended with a grand Tea. This same Quarterly Meeting noted that the price asked for the plot of land for the building of the Colerne chapel "was exorbitant and we therefore decline it". However, about 1890 land was offered at Star Corner and the local Methodists raised £480 for the building of the Chapel in 1895.

Sunday School Affairs

Sunday School Anniversaries were important events. Children were required to sing and recite, and proud and nervous parents looked on. Sunday School Teachers after weeks of preparation and practice, agonised over the performances. Slightly less worrying was the annual Sunday School Outing. The sea-side ones must have started in the 1920s and usually Weston-super-Mare was the venue. After the excitement of the journey in the charabanc, there were the endless golden sands, the pier, the donkeys and paddling in the murky waters (Dads rolled up their Sunday trousers, dresses could be tucked in knickers without raising a parental frown!). In the 1930s organised Tea was taken at Brown's Cafe. Fish and chips at Coffin's completed the day of delight.

The subscription list dated 1896 for the new harmonium, costing £18 10s 0d from Duck, Son & Pinker, contains many well-known Colerne names. There was a Service of Song to dedicate the instrument and other expenses were: Sheet Music 4s 6d, Stamps 2s 6d,

Stationery 3d, Printing Bills 2s 7d, Washing cloths 9d, cleaning Chapel 2s 6d.

From the turn of the century worship continued and, one hopes, made an impact for good on the life of the village. There were occasions of rejoicing and times of sadness. From brief written references and Church memorials we note the tragic impact of two World Wars. There are many memories. In the latter years, the sharing of the Methodist Covenant Service with our Anglican friends and others is one which will not be forgotten. Schemes of union with the Anglican Church in 1966 and 1980 fell through. The Methodist Church at Colerne failed in its outreach and was closed by common consent of its members but one hopes that its witness over the years is not a total failure.

The Revd Sally Shaw, preaching the last service in October 1984, reminded us that sometimes we had to be "broken to be made anew". The Anglican, Evangelical and Christian Fellowship Churches proclaim the same Gospel in different ways – may the time come when in the prophetic words of Charles Wesley, "names and sects and parties fall . . . . . ".

Fig 12   Methodist Sunday school outing to Weston, 1947

Fig 13 Methodist Nativity play, 1974

Independent Churches in Colerne
1670–1989

This chapter has been compiled by Gordon Maynard with the help of material supplied by Norman Alford (Independent and Evangelical Churches), Ebenezer Knight and Margaret Greenman (Strict Baptist Church) and Paul Cooke (Colerne Christian Fellowship)

Individuals in many villages probably regard their own village as unique in some particular way. As regards non-conformist history, Colerne is indeed unique. We do not find just an Independent Chapel and a Baptist Chapel, but two chapels whose beginnings were bound up together as an Independent Church and then divided into two, and then three, separate churches, each of which in itself differed from mainstream non-conformism. To understand this better we need first to give a broad account of non-conformity in England.

The Church and dissent

Although the power of the Roman Catholic church in England was broken by Henry VIII (1491–1574), this was mainly for his own ends and the English 'Reformation' brought little change in theology. True 'Independency' in church worship stems from the same period, but from the movements in Europe of Martin Luther (1483–1546) and John Calvin (1509–64), whose central doctrine asserted that only the elect were predestined to eternal salvation. While the Lutheran church believed that power to suppress schism should be in the hands of the secular authorities, Calvin evolved a form of government in which the whole life of the community was under church control. From these massive growths there sprang other more tender, but not timid, plants: Independents (Congregational) and Baptists. The earliest of the latter were 'Arminians' who believed (unlike Calvin) that salvation was open to all mankind.

Under Elizabeth I the Church of England was firmly protestant, with Calvinistic leanings. Its theology was based on Archbishop Cranmer's prayerbook of 1553, with the monarch as its earthly head. At this time the first Puritans (the name dates from 1564) emerged. They desired to abolish religious ceremony and they doubted the biblical authority for bishops, but they worked for change from within the Church.

Independents

It is difficult to portray adequately the debt we owe to the Independents of the sixteenth and seventeenth centuries. Much of our secular, as well as our religious, freedom comes from the valiant struggles of these tiny groups who dared to protest their right to conduct their religious worship according to the dictates of their conscience, *and* that others of different persuasions should have like freedom. These people held to simple beliefs based on the Bible and, what was dangerous treason, on the conviction that no monarch or government could exercise authority over a gathering of Christians – a 'Church'.

They had suffered imprisonment and torture, even hanging, under Elizabeth and their lot was little better during the reigns of James I and Charles I (1603–49). Laud (Archbishop of Canterbury, 1633–40) with his 'High Church' Arminianism alienated the Puritans, but his wrath fell particularly on all forms of Independency. Fines, torture and imprisonment were meted out: but persecution breeds faith.

The emergence of the Baptist Church

To avoid severe repression and persecution, some adherents of the Independent movement in England fled to the Netherlands. Here a group led by John Smyth (died c 1612) formed a Baptist Church which believed in adult rather than infant baptism. He and his supporters may have been the first to believe that there should be *total* religious freedom.

Later, in England, a follower of John Smyth, Thomas Helwys, formed the first Arminian General Baptist congregation at Spitalfields, London, 1612. But about 1633 some Calvinistic Independents under Samuel Eaton formed a group rejecting baptism in the established church and probably *any* form of infant baptism. In 1638 a group, quite definitely rejecting infant baptism, formed the first Particular Baptist Church with John Spilsbury as pastor. Between 1640 and 1648 Presbyterian Puritanism dominated the state church with little sympathy for any sects. The Model Army intervened and from 1648 there was greater toleration, many Baptists holding high office in the State.

Further struggles

Charles II, who was anxious to protect his Catholic subjects, sought to implement his supreme power in ecclesiastical matters by means of a Declaration of Indulgence (1672) which repealed laws against Catholics and Dissenters, but Parliament was infuriated by the King's unconstitutional methods and the Declaration was withdrawn. The Test Act of 1673 again severely repressed Dissenters (especially Romanists). They were anxious to claim that they were loyal citizens, but they fervently fought for religious freedom.

Under James II, churchmen and non-conformists were temporarily united against the king when he threw the Archbishop of Canterbury and six bishops into the Tower in his struggle to gain ascendancy over both the Church and Parliament. James lost, and the Presbyterian Calvinist William of Orange and his wife Mary came to the throne in the 'Glorious Revolution' of 1688. Compulsory attendance of the Church of England was abolished. The Toleration Act of 1689 provided for the registration of all places of religious assembly by bishops, archdeacons or magistrates, at a charge of 6d. This was not compulsory; but earlier Acts against Dissenters were not repealed, and they were sometimes used against groups whose meeting places had not been registered.

Independency in Colerne

We do not know what prompted some ordinary Colerne people to forsake the established church except a desire for freedom of religious worship, but records include an application for a Meeting House Certificate as early as 15th July 1690. The meeting place was described as "the house of Joan Hooke, widow" and the application was signed by Zachariah Millerd, Anthony Drewett, the mark of Thomas Grinway, Richard Aust, David Grinway, Obadiah Cheltenham, Henry Jones, Daniel Grinway and John Jones.

There was, of course, greater freedom of conscience under William and Mary, but there remained severe restrictions on such Dissenters. They were disqualified from holding any office in the State, they could not bury their dead in their own graveyards or gain admission to the Universities of Oxford or Cambridge. Nevertheless Colerne continued to throw up dissenting groups and further Certificates were granted in 1695 (for a Presbyterian group), 1719, 1797 and 1799 – the last of these was for "the house of Thomas Bethel" (Independent) and was signed by Thomas Aust, James Tanner, Mary Knight, "housekeepers in Colerne".

The Independent Chapel

A Certificate of 26th August 1824 is of special interest because it refers to a "building which has been recently built"; it is signed by Thomas Aust and Charles Butler. This Independent Chapel (in Chapel Path) had a Trust Deed dated 1st March 1824 (registered by the Charity Commissioners) which was held by the Congregational Union, and it had links with two Bath Chapels, the Countess of Huntingdon's Connexion at the Paragon and the Argyle Street Congregational Chapel.

Tension, theological differences – the Strict Baptist Church

There was a strong Baptist leaning among some members of the Independent Chapel who were drawn to the ministry of William Gadsby and John Warburton of Trowbridge. By the 1850s, a number became concerned about believers' baptism which is not part of Congregational practice, and in 1851 thirteen of them were baptised in the brook at Long Dean near Castle Combe.

Further baptisms took place, and those of the Baptist persuasion gained a majority in the Church. This gave offence to the Congregational Union. Finally the Trustees ordered the senior Deacon, Reuben Aust, to give up the keys of the Chapel. The Church records comment "we neither looked for nor expected such a calamity to overtake us".

The Deacons refused to give up the keys and the case was taken to the High Court of Chancery in April 1863, where the Judge decided against the Baptists, who had to deliver up the keys and also meet the costs of £200 (which must have been a tremendous sum for such village folk to find). However, their plight reached the ears of a Mr Aikman who resided in India and he presented them with £500 which was entrusted to Samuel May. Help and encouragement were received from a Baptist pastor of Bradford-on-Avon. In 1866 the majority left the Independent Chapel and met in a barn which was fitted up for worship. This barn still stands and is the one which has recently been renovated at Ragge Farm. In 1867 they obtained a site in the main street of the village for which £115 was paid. On 9th May the foundation stone was laid, and in November of that year the Providence Strict Baptist Chapel was opened by John Warburton. The name 'Providence' derives from the conviction that God had wonderfully supplied all their needs.

The Chapel was well attended at that time, and in the years that followed a large Sunday school was formed under the leadership of Mrs Emma Knight. A highlight of the year was the annual treat and prize-giving day when the children were entertained with buns and other goodies and played games at Mr Knight's farm, in the paddock where Grocyn Close now stands. One year they ventured further afield and hired a charabanc to take them to Weston-super-Mare; but the Sunday school work seems to have come to an end a few years after the death of Mrs Knight in 1925.

No pastor was appointed until 1976. Up to that time services were taken week by week by various visiting preachers. These were often fetched from Box station by pony and trap.

Mr Samuel Sheppard moved up with his family from Box, and had a lot to do with the general running of the chapel, and for years he started the tunes without the aid of even a pitch pipe. It was noted that the congregation always sang well in four-part harmony, a fact that was true right up to recent years, although by that time it was helped along by the addition of an organ.

As more members were added to the church, baptismal services continued to take place in the open, first at Long Dean, then at Widdenham and later in the mill stream at West Kington. The last

Fig 14   Providence chapel, Colerne

baptism recorded there was that of Mary Knight, formerly of Chapel Path, on 31st July 1932. There was in those days considerable antagonism to baptism by immersion and it was noted at the time, with great thankfulness to God, that it rained throughout, thereby keeping at home those who had threatened to disrupt the service. Baptisms after that time were held in other local chapels 'borrowed' for the occasion, until in 1971, the members of Providence chapel built their own baptistry.

In 1960, one of the members, Mr E J Knight, was invited to a pastorate in America and stayed there until 1976. On many of his annual visits home he conducted baptismal services as more were added to the church, amongst whom were children, grandchildren and others of his family. After his return in 1976 the church called him to be their pastor – the first in their history. One of the last baptismal services to be held in the chapel was on 1st February 1982 when he baptised eight more of his own family. The pastorate came to an end in January 1984.

Fig 15   Baptist Sunday school 'treat', 1929

STRICT BAPTIST CHURCH

An Extract of the Articles of Faith

The divine inspiration of the Holy Scriptures; there is One living and true God with three Persons in the Godhead, Father, Son and Holy Ghost; the election by the Father of a certain number of the human race to everlasting salvation through Jesus Christ; all men are born in sin and involved in Adam's transgression and unable and unwilling to deliver themselves; the Lord Jesus Christ being really man and truly God, did suffer, bleed, die and rise for the salvation of His people, and now intercedes in Heaven for them; His redemption is special and particular; it is the work of the Holy Ghost to call, sanctify and lead the people of God from nature to grace and from grace to glory; justification in the sight of God is by faith in Christ Jesus; the final perseverance of all true believers; the resurrection of the body, the judgement of the world by our Lord Jesus Christ, the eternal blessedness of the righteous and the eternal punishment of the wicked; Baptism and the Lord's Supper are Ordinances of Christ to be continued till His second coming; Baptism by immersion of those who have come to saving faith in the Lord Jesus, the Lord's Supper where saints commemorate the sacrificial death of Christ for their salvation.

From this congregation there emerged a majority group calling themselves Colerne Christian Fellowship. In April 1986 the chapel building was vacated, as the Fellowship no longer worshipped according to the terms of the original Trust Deed. Those concerned wait until they feel that God directs a course of action.

The Independent Chapel and the Colerne Evangelical Church

We can now return to the continuing life and progress of the Independent Chapel. The traumatic upheaval of the split did not daunt their faith or fervour. On 6th February 1867 they found it expedient to re-establish their Articles of Faith and Qualifications for Church Membership (firmly based on scripture). An extract of the principal qualifications appears in a separate panel on page 46. Although tied to the Congregational Church by their Deed, it is evident that they were strongly 'independent' and governed their own affairs.

Fig 16   Evangelical chapel, Colerne

The life of the Church over the years is well illustrated by the following extracts from the Church Minutes:

1867   At a Church Meeting held 6 February it was resolved that church members be allowed to bury without fee.
Any other person wishing to do so shall pay a fee of 6d (sixpence).

1868   At a Church Meeting held on 17 February it was resolved that any person occupying a seat will be expected to pay for the same within 14 days after the quarter day or the Deacons will be at liberty to re-let the same.

1869   20 July the Revd E Edwards of the Free Church Calne preached the anniversary sermon. After which a public meeting was held in the burial ground. Addresses were given by the Revd Darby, Edwards, Bailey and Millard.

1870   At a Church Meeting held on 21 January it was resolved that any person belonging to the High Baptist Church in this village should be allowed to bury their dead in the burial ground belonging to the Independent Chapel but that the church should be consulted as to the officiating minister.

1874   6 July the Revd Bailey of Crockerton preached the anniversary sermon. There was a very large congregation present, 400 partook of a good tea. A public meeting was held in the burial ground in the evening.

1882   Revd B Rodes of Wootton Bassett entered the pastorate of the Batheaston and Colerne Churches 1 January.

During the period 1841–1924 the church also came under the care of Argyle Chapel, Bath.

1924   Renovation of chapel £32 4s 7d.

1933   Installation of gas lighting £7 0s 0d.
April. It was proposed that the cleaner be paid 12s 0d per quarter.

The following items from the financial accounts of 1867 are also of interest:

> Seat money £2 1s 0d; Candles 4s 6d; Faggots [wood] 4s 6d; Window blinds 6s 6d; Gifts to the poor 9s 6d; Lodging for preachers 2s 0d; Coal 2s 0d; Wine 2s 0d; Wood and coal 3s 6d; 2 Babies graves 5s 0d; Tins for oil 2s 0d; Tapers 6d; 1 Small lamp 3s 5d; 8 Large lamps £5 16s 3d; 1 Doz New Testaments 4s 0d; 1 Chimney pot and putting up 4s 6d.

In 1932 an important event took place. On 21st November representatives of the Wilts and East Somerset Congregational Union met with church members to invite Mr H L Matthews of Biddestone to become lay preacher. He took up his duties on 4th December 1932.

In 1934 Mr Leslie Fletcher became Church Secretary and shortly afterwards Sunday School Superintendent. Apart from the war years he served the church faithfully right up to his death in 1982. He was a lay preacher and well known and acceptable in many churches in the area. His warm personality and sense of humour endeared him to many. During this time Mr Henry Aust became church organist and he has carried that responsibility through to the present day. He has also served as a Sunday school teacher and church treasurer.

Prior to 1932, the Church continued to follow the Congregational practice of infant baptism, but there are no references to baptism by immersion before the appointment of Pastor Matthews. This was plainly not a condition of membership or of partaking of the Lord's Supper. There was no baptistry at the church. The first recollection of such baptism taking place was in 1942 at Widcombe Baptist Church, Bath, with various church members/believers going through the waters of baptism during the following years. In 1963 the first outdoor baptism was held at the home of Mr and Mrs N Alford, using the garden swimming pool. Between 1963 and 1975 nine believers were baptised there by the Revd Timothy Alford of London.

It is appropriate here to note other important milestones in the life of the church. On 8th September 1970 Pastor H L Matthews resigned after thirty-eight years of faithful service. On 24th November 1972 the Wilts and East Somerset Congregational Union retired from the

46 The Village on the Hill

trusteeship of the Independent Chapel and it was thenceforth administered by those elected from the church membership. In 1974 the name of the chapel was changed to Colerne Evangelical Church.

COLERNE EVANGELICAL CHURCH

An Extract of the Articles of Faith

"To these and quite a few more the Church holds dear"

The first recorded Minutes of the Chapel are dated 6th February 1867. They lay down the qualifications for Church membership, all of them scripture based. Here is an extract:

That they [persons seeking church membership] hold no doctrine contrary to the fundamental truths of Christianity such as the being of God, the doctrine of Trinity in unity, the Divinity and Incarnation of Christ and the mystery of His person as God Man. The fullness and all sufficiency of His work and offices. God's everlasting purpose and covenant. The guilt and corruption of all mankind by the fall of Adam. The justification of a sinner before God by faith alone. The necessity of the work of the Holy Spirit to regenerate and sanctify those who believe to Salvation and to dispose them to walk becoming the Gospel in all holy conversation. The perfection of the law of God as our rule of duty and our eternal obligations to obedience and conformity to it.

The following additions are extracted from a recent Church Constitution (1989):

Membership of the church shall be open to those who:

1. Give satisfactory evidence of being born again, of true repentance towards God and of having faith in the Lord Jesus Christ.

2. Have been baptised by immersion upon profession of faith in Christ (consideration is given to persons who for health reasons are not able to be immersed and to any person who has made a confession of faith in Christ by effusion of water, provided such persons accept our teaching and practice of baptism by immersion).

Returning to the account of baptisms, on 10th April 1982 Mr Paul Stinchcombe, a member of the Evangelical church was baptised in Providence Chapel, there being no baptistry in the Evangelical church

Fig 17   Digging the baptistry, Evangelical chapel

Fig 18   The 'Good News Club', 1950s

at that time. In 1983 the members decided to build their own baptistry, but after removal of flooring it was found necessary to renew all timber work. This work as well as the building of the baptistry was all carried out by various members. The first persons to be baptised in the new baptistry were Andrew Stinchcombe and others, in August 1984. Over subsequent years, numerous baptisms have taken place, usually performed by the Deacons.

The pastorate was taken up by Pastor A Donnelly on 6 January 1985. The chapel itself is beautifully appointed and continues to be lovingly cared for.

Colerne Christian Fellowship

The pastorate of the Strict Baptist Church having come to an end in January 1984, its members continued to meet together without any formal leadership. However, a meeting held in December 1984 proved to be a significant turning point in the life of the church and its aims for the future. Mr Paul Cooke was asked to take the office of Pastor. Shortly afterwards, although still continuing to meet in Providence Chapel, the church felt the need to dissociate itself from the past and to present Christianity to the community in a fresh, vital way. To this end it was agreed that the church fellowship meeting in Providence Chapel would now call itself Colerne Christian Fellowship and would seek, not to isolate itself, but rather to reach out to fellow Christians in the village.

During 1985, the Fellowship began to feel that the building in which it worshipped would be more useful if it were refurbished. However, the Trustees were unhappy about changes to the fabric or fittings, and it further became clear that certain aspects of the Fellowship's mode of worship were not compatible with the terms of the original deed. Because of this, they felt that they should vacate Providence Chapel and so, from April 1986, began meeting on Sunday afternoons in the Parish Church Hall. In May 1988 the venue changed to the Scout Hall.

In September 1988 a number of young people became involved with the Colerne Youth Club, working alongside other villagers.

Having been in existence for four years, the Fellowship began to feel the need to reach out to the village, and it was decided to hold a Mission early in 1989. Colin Stephenson, a Scripture Union Children's Evangelist, spent a week in the village holding meetings daily for children and a number of events for families. Following this and the enthusiastic response to the children's meetings, it was decided to form the King's Club for 7–11 year olds, meeting weekly. The Fellowship is also much involved with the Christian Men's Network and shows videos monthly on all aspects of manhood. As a group of believers, the Fellowship sees itself working alongside other Christian groups in the village and, to this end, has met several times with the Anglicans.

COLERNE CHRISTIAN FELLOWSHIP

Statement of Faith and Belief

1. We believe the Bible to be the infallible authoritative Word of God.
2. We believe that there is one God eternally existent in Three Persons: Father, Son and Holy Spirit.
3. We believe in the Deity of our Lord Jesus Christ, His Virgin Birth, His Sinless Life, His Miracles and His Vicarious Death and Resurrection.
4. We believe that He ascended to the right hand of the Father.
5. We believe that man is born in sin and separated from God and that he needs, by repentance and faith, to come to a personal knowledge of the saving power of Jesus.
6. We believe that the Holy Spirit was sent to indwell the believer and anoint him with power for service.
7. We believe in the Gifts and Graces of the Holy Spirit and in the spiritual unity of all believers.

Qualifications for Membership

We believe our main purpose and commission is to reach out and share the Gospel of Jesus Christ that all men may know, and come to a knowledge of, the saving power of Jesus. We therefore maintain that experiencing this is the qualification for membership in His church.

Breaking of Bread and Baptism

We believe it is the right and privilege of every believer to enjoy and partake of, the Breaking of Bread; we would welcome any to join with us who named Jesus as Lord.

In accordance with our Lord's command to preach the Gospel and make disciples, we believe that all believers should be baptised as a visible expression of a commitment to the Lord.

Conclusion

As a generalisation, one of the marks of these particular churches is 'simplicity'. That is simplicity in the forms of worship and lack of special forms of dress or ritual in the conduct of services. Extempore prayer is another distinguishing feature. Church government is administered by elected deacons under the care of a pastor, who is unlikely to be a full-time paid minister.

Simplicity must not be taken to mean lack of order. Faith and order are held to be vitally important in the witness of these 'independent' churches.

Sources

Oliver R W, *The Strict Baptist Churches of England*, Fauconberg Press.
Wiltshire Record Office, various papers.

Monumental Inscriptions

Sandie Waite

I first became aware of the need for monumental inscriptions to be transcribed when the Federation of Family History Societies launched a nationwide campaign. Gravestones were rapidly deteriorating and the information on them was being lost for all time.

Having first gained permission from the Rector, I began my project in the late summer of 1986. I first made a brief survey of the churchyard and was pleased to see how well kept it was, thanks to a small group of volunteers who regularly see to grass cutting and to the caring relatives who attend to the graves themselves.

With the stones facing east I found the best time of day to work was in the morning making use of natural light. This was very important with the older stones as they were often worn and difficult to read.

I made a start at the front (west side) of the churchyard where the most recent stones stand. Most of these bear just one or two names, dates and a few words of endearment.

Their condition was so good that in just a couple of weeks I had rapidly worked my way along the north wall as far as the vault. Progress then began to slow down. This was due to many things: age and the elements taking their toll made reading difficult, and the style of writing had changed too, so extra care had to be taken in recording the data accurately. I also found the older the stone the more information it gave: some I found had up to three or four generations on them.

My husband Phil became a willing volunteer and was a great help to me. He very carefully used a brush and water to clean off dirt and lichen. Where overgrown ivy clung this had to be clipped with secateurs before it could be removed. Sadly many of the old stones had

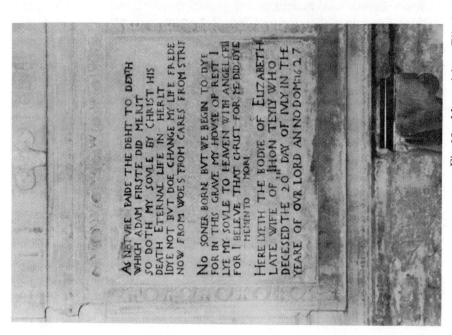

Fig 19   Memorials to Elizabeth Teyly and the Jaggard family

deteriorated beyond recognition but, despite this, 414 in the church-yard were recorded along with another 30 inside the church and a further six in the Evangelical church, totalling 450, spanning 360 years back to 1627.

Inside the church posed a problem. Many 'tablets' are high up above the vestry door where lighting is poor, and Phil had to read these by torch light perched on top of a ladder. Added to this, many are written in Latin and had to be translated.

These stones give us a great deal of information about relationships, occupations, place of residence, dates and ages, and epitaphs tell us of the people themselves. These people are our village history. Our earliest recording of 1627 is to be found inside the church and is of Elizabeth Tiley, an old village name still to be found to-day, as are Hulbert going back to 1653, Aust 1771 and Sumsion 1775.

Where occupations are given they give us a broad outline of what village life was like. We found seven yeomen of c1735 engaged in agriculture, four members of the Drewitt family of c1750 were clothiers, and Charles and Amelia Jaggard of c1900 were "teachers of Colerne School". Several members of the Ford family of c1767 were stone masons, builders and 'statuaries' of Bath.

Jonathan Southward of c1727 was a butcher and his epitaph reads:

By these inscriptions be it understood
my occupation was in shedding blood.
And many a beast by me was weekly slain,
Hunger to ease and mortals to maintain.
Now here I rest from sin and sorrow free
By means of him who shed his blood for me.

John Bedford died in 1825 aged 22 years, the victim of violence. His stone reads:

Farewell my dearest friends, I could no longer stay
t'was wicked men with fatal blows that took my life away.
It was a long and tedious time, I had to mourn and grieve
t'was past physicians art and skill my blessed life to save.
You young men pray think of me as I am in my grave
Shun the path of wickedness if you think your life to save.
Farewell you all my dearest friends I have no more to say
Let wicked men repent in haste and prepare for a blessed day.

Fig 20   Memorial to Ford family

The Sumsion family were very prominent in the eighteenth and nineteenth centuries and many members were obviously held in esteem as they are recorded as "worthy and useful", "In living adorned the character of wife, mother and friend and who dying was the humble expectant of a blessed immortability" and "They exhibited

Fig 22   Mullins memorial in Evangelical churchyard

Fig 21   Memorial to John Bedford

while living an example of benevolence and integrity, their death was sincerely deplored by their relatives and friends".

Forty stones stand tall and erect in military fashion and belong to servicemen. Six bear the date 6th July 1965. They recall the tragic event when over 40 officers and airmen were killed near Colerne airfield when their Hastings aircraft crashed shortly after take off. Many others fought and gave their lives in the 1939–45 war, some as far away from home as Canada and New Zealand. The village lost thirteen of its own men in 1914–18 and a further eleven during 1939–45.

Fig 23   Military gravestones

I found the project I had undertaken to be very interesting, worth while and on the whole enjoyable. Despite writer's cramp and cold feet (it was December before we completed), it was a peaceful environment to work in and the few interruptions I had were from people who took an interest in what I was doing and often had a story to relate.

Fig 24   Replica of Saxon cross in churchyard

However, one incident sticks out in my mind. I like to think of myself as a logical person not given to fanciful thought or too much imagination, but one day in the south-east corner of the churchyard something brought my work to a halt.

The sun was shining brightly in a cloudless blue sky and the air was clear, but not a sound could be heard. No birds, no noise of traffic, no voices, nothing; just the awareness that someone from behind was watching. I turned round but there was no one there of course. It was very unnerving and probably lasted not more than a couple of minutes when the church clock struck the hour of 12 noon, sending roosting birds into noisy flight, followed by the excited chatter of young children as they left the adjoining play-group, breaking that silent spell. That morning I was happy to go home and 'call it a day!'

Colerne History Group holds a copy of Sandie Waite's complete inventory of the monumental inscriptions. This is available for inspection, and photocopies of entries can be provided at cost. Postal enquiries should be accompanied by return postage plus a nominal contribution to other expenses.

Four Old Village Names and Families

Joan Platt

In all the old village records, four names appear over and over again: Aust, Sumsion, Tiley and Tanner. There are variations of the spelling of the first three, but Tanner remains the same through the centuries.

Aust appears as Auste, with an e, in the first four marriage entries (1561–74); in 1651 it is Ast, but thereafter always Aust.

Sumsion has many variations: in the 1500s it seems to be Sympson; after that it is Sumsion, Sumtion or Symsion, but after the middle of the eighteenth century it is almost invariably Sumsion.

In the Taxation Lists of 1576, there were 22 names from Colerne three of which were Roberte Auste, Richard Sympson and Thomas Sympson. The first two were assessed to £3, with a first instalment of 5s, and Thomas Sympson to 20s with a first instalment of 2s 8d. So they were both established families in Colerne in Elizabeth I's reign.

Tiley also has many spellings. The earliest record of the family in the village is on the north wall of the Church: a memorial to Elizabeth, late wife of John Teyly, dated July 1627. In 1674 the name is recorded in the Marriage Register as Tily, Joshop Tily marrying Ane Lediat. In 1701 it becomes Tyly, and from then on it varies between Tyley, Tily, Tilee, Tyly and Tilley.

All four names appear in the list of Overseers of the Poor from 1688 onwards, when available records start. The names of Thomas and Richard Aust, Nicholas Tanner and Thomas and Samuel Sumsion are all mentioned. The Widow Tanner was the first recorded woman overseer in 1709, Thomas Tyly was appointed in 1727, William Tyly in 1730, and Mary Aust's name appears in 1735. So they were families of some standing in the village, as overseers were required to look after the sick and poor, and the maintenance of hedges and lanes.

The names Aust, Sumsion and Tiley appear together in the overseers' record of 13th March 1714 of the "Expenses relating to last sickness and death of Joseph Tyly", when he was cared for by William Sumsion and the coffin was made by Richard Aust. He was laid out by Edward Dyor, and "people to carry him to the grave" were paid 3s 0d. At that time the law required bodies to be buried in wool, and an affidavit was signed to that effect.

In the Colerne Enclosure award of 1787, two of the families, Aust and Tiley, received enclosures: Thomas Aust was awarded 43 acres, and Ferdinando Aust, Richard Aust and Thomas Tiley all received unspecified smaller areas.

Through the centuries these four families have played their part in the village as farmers, builders, stone masons, carpenters, agricultural workers, as well as being innkeepers, maltsters and shopkeepers. Through hard times and good times the families have survived, and have their place in our village history.

The Austs

The name Aust is believed to be German. The original family must have come over to England very early on – possibly escaping from religious persecution as there is a tradition that they were Huguenots – as the first Auste in the old Marriage Register is Robert Auste who married Joane Edwards in 1561. Five months later Alis Auste married John Edwards: it sounds a close family arrangement.

There were two more Auste weddings in that century. In 1571 John Auste married Alis Nott and in 1574 Elnor Auste and John Woodroffe were married.

In the next century there is an inventory of the goods and money of another Eleanor Auste, taken in 1635, which reads:

A true Inventory. . . . . of all the goodes and money of Eleanor Auste, late deceased, taken and praysed by Anthoney Bennett, Nicholaus Auste and Richard Bennett, the twenty six day of May 1635 within the parish of Collerne:

	£	s	d
Imprimis: Two platters		4	0
Item: Foure sasers and one pewter dish		ij[2]	0

Item: One goune att		10	0
Item: Two wastkoates		ij[2]	0
Item: Two aprons, one smok one pillowbe[re] [pillowcase]			
with some other smalle linning			
clothes, praysed att		10	0
Item: One box, three silver rings in tin,			
together with a silk girdle and some			
other small things, praysed at		4	0
Item: A bonde the some whereof comes too	7	12	4
The totall some	£9	4	4
The funerall expences xij s[12s]			

From writing in Latin on the bottom of the Inventory, it can be gathered that her father was John Auste, and her brother and sister (minors), Richard and Mary, were to benefit from her goods and money.

In the great fire in Colerne in 1774, Daniel Aust was recorded as a woolcomber, and lost chattels to the value of £13 4s 3d.

In the Aust family tree, the unusual name of Ferdinando appears. He was baptised in 1680 and was the son, by an unnamed first wife, of Richard Aust. It would be interesting to know if she was Spanish or Portuguese and wanted her son to have this un-English name. He was a copyholder of Ragge Farm, then known as the Homestead, and may have lived there, as in the List of Persons in the County of Wiltshire who were qualified to act as jurors in 1736 his name was among the 23 from Colerne. His eldest grandson, also Ferdinando, had fourteen children, though not all survived. The eldest was David Aust who was a builder and built the bridge over the river Avon on North Parade in Bath in 1836. There is a bronze plaque at the end of the bridge saying David Aust was the builder.

Another son was Samuel Aust who was a victualler. His second wife was Ann Dix, and a family story tells how her father was killed by highwaymen, left on the roadside, and his horse stolen. They had seven children, Obadiah, Rhoda, Abijah, Elijah, Abigail (known as Tabitha), Jabez and Elisha. Abijah and Elijah (known as Bije and Lije) went to America and were in the American Civil War. There is a photograph of them in uniform with their mother, Ann, taken in Chatham. Had she journeyed there to see them off on their ship?

Abigail (Tabitha) married Henry Gaisford and had a shop in Bath Road, now No. 13, as well as looking after ten children. Their grandson was Samuel Gaisford, the nurseryman and sweet pea specialist, who had the large nurseries in Bath Road where the Firs Estate is now.

The eldest son of David, the bridge builder, was Daniel, a stone mason, who lived at 11 Bath Road with his wife Sarah and their six children, who were all baptised in the Independent Congregational Chapel in Chapel Path. Two of their sons, Elijah and Elisha went to Australia in 1853: Elijah with his wife Emma to Ballarat, Victoria, in search of gold, and their ten children were all born in the goldfields around Ballarat. One of their descendants corresponds with Mr and Mrs Henry Aust in Bath Road. Elisha went to Perth, Western Australia, and his descendants have visited Colerne looking for their roots.

David's second son was another Ferdinando, and the third son, Richard, was a builder like his father. His initials are on a house in Moon Close, dated 1825. He was married to Sarah Rose, and they had nine children all baptised in the Independent Chapel, and called by biblical names, the first three being Martha, Mary and Lazarus! The fourth son was David who worked on the land and married his cousin Ann Aust, who was a dressmaker.

Thomas Aust, a grandson of the first Ferdinando, was a yeoman farmer, who died in 1821, and is buried with many of his family in the Aust family vault in the churchyard near the west door of the church. He had ten children by his first wife Mary, and four by Meliscent, his second wife. His son Daniel was a yeoman farmer, and also his grandson Charles.

With such large families, it is not surprising that in the 1841 census there were ten Aust households in Colerne, including Sarah, aged 75, recorded as a "lodging-house keeper"; in 1851 there were twelve households, and in 1861 there were thirteen. They were mostly living in Bath Road, Moon Close and Star Corner. No wonder that end of the village was known as Aust's End!

They were farmers (at Eastrip and Elm Farm in Bath Road), builders, masons, journeymen maltsters, shopkeepers, coal and corn merchants, bakers and a basketmaker, and in 1878 George Aust was a

Fig 26   Ann Aust with Elijah and Abijah at Chatham

Fig 25   Samuel and Ann Aust with son

steward at the Rocks, the large house just outside the village on the Fosseway. He lived at 4 Bath Road, and had a new front of faced stone put on his house, as can be seen today.

For some years from 1855, Edwin Aust worked as a carpenter in a little shed up the path to Rockfield, and in the early 1900s Frederick Aust was Secretary of the Conservative Club in Colerne.

In the 1860s some of the members of the Independent Chapel, including Reuben Aust who was the Senior Deacon, decided to break away and build their own Chapel. This building, dated 1867, is named Providence Chapel and stands in the High Street. It was all built by voluntary labour and two of the Austs were among the builders: their initials RA and DA can be seen carved on an outside wall.

After the first World War, Colerne villagers were woken on Christmas morning by Sidney Aust, from Bath Road, playing "Christians Awake, Salute the Happy Morn" on his accordion, and there are people in the village today who remember it as a wonderful way to start Christmas.

Another Aust, Evelyn Elizabeth, went to Canada, but Colerne held such happy memories for her that she asked that when she died her ashes should be sent back to Colerne and this tablet be placed in the Church, and she sent money for it to be done:

IN MEMORY OF
EVELYN ELIZABETH MICHAEL
NÉE AUST
WHOSE HAPPY CHILDHOOD
WAS ASSOCIATED WITH THIS
PARISH AND CHURCH
1880–1964

Although there is only one Aust family left now in the village, there are very many descendants of this large family still living here.

The Sumsions

The Sumsions were an established family in Colerne in Elizabeth I's reign. The first record of the name in the old Marriage Register is of John Collyns marrying Mary Sympsion in 1560; more follow in the

1600s, but in the 1700s there are 52 entries under the name, an average of about one Sumsion wedding every two years!

Many of the Sumsions were stone masons, and the most famous among these was Thomas Sumsion, who was born around 1672, and was an architect and banker mason. His name appears in the Biographical Dictionary of British Architects, and he is famed for carrying on medieval designs into the eighteenth century. When the existing tower and spire of the church at Dursley in Gloucestershire fell down, he designed and built the new tower in 1707, basing it on the design of Colerne church tower, and the contractors Barker and Sumsion received £500 "for building the tower". In 1730 he designed the Gothic tower of Holy Cross church at Sherston, with battlements and pinnacles, for which he was paid £1 15s 0d for his "draught". There are also examples of his stone carving at Kings Weston, near Bristol, now the Headquarters of the Avon and Somerset Constabulary. On the north front roof are two large elaborately carved urns, and the contract for these, dated 19th April 1717, reads "I, Thomas Sumsion, do hereby propose to provide Horse Carriadge to Kings Weston and setting up a pair of Urnes six foot high according to a draft by me drawn for Four Pounds the Pair. But if made according to the same draft of seven foot high at Four Pounds ten shillings the Pair". He died in October 1744, aged 72, and was buried in Colerne churchyard. His will was proved in October 1745 by his widow, Joan Sumsion, and he left goods worth £329, including "working tools in the shop", and a writing desk in the kitchen. He would have been the Thomas Sumsion who was appointed overseer for the year 1717.

Another mason was Samuel Sumsion, who left a will in 1734 describing himself as "Stonecutter of the parrish of Collern". He left to his two brothers Thomas and Richard "£100 of good and lawful money of Great Britain . . . . upon trust only to be divided by them or their heirs between my three children in equal shares viz. Joseph, Elizabeth and Thomas or their heirs". Joseph and Thomas were also to have all his "Waring Apparel both lining and woollen in equal shares" and his daughter Elizabeth was to have all "woman's apparel, both lining and woollen which remains of my wife's deceased". To his son Samuel, who was to be his sole executor, he bequeathed "all and every my messuages, lands, tenements and hereditaments whatsoever and wheresoever". He also required his executor to find and provide sufficient meat, drink, washing and lodgings for his three children aforesaid . . . . . for the space of twelve months after his decease. It would seem that Samuel was the son of a first marriage, as he was old enough to be the executor of his father's will. But what happened to the three children after that first twelve months? Another story, if the pages of village history could be turned back. Four years after the date of the will, there is a Samuel Sumsion marrying Phillipa Ford in the Marriage Register, but it is not possible to identify accurately all the Samuels, as it seems to have been a very popular name in the family, just as Michael was later in the century.

One Michael Sumsion was buried in the churchyard in 1775, with a long inscription on his gravestone:

> Whilst pale disease upon his vitals preyed
> His strength exhausted and his frame decayed
> With painful steps life lingered to the grave
> When human skill had lost the power to save
> Yet full kind Heaven disposed of his virtuous mind
> To live with patience and die refined.

and two more Michaels lie side by side under beautifully carved headstones. The dates would suggest that they are father and son. The later one has an inscription "Sacred to the memory of that useful and worthy man Michael Sumsion of this place who died June 20th 1786 age 60 years", and his wife Mary is described as "who living adorned the character of the wife the friend the mother and who dying was the humble expectant of a blessed immortability. Through Jesus Christ she departed this life September 18th 1802 aged 71 years", sixteen years after her husband.

Inside the Church on the north wall of the Lady Chapel there are memorials to other Sumsions: Charles and his wife Ann, dying within six months of each other, aged 52 and 53 (1808–9). The inscription reads "They exhibited while living an example of benevolence and integrity. Their death was sincerely deplored by their relatives and friends. But the sorrow occasioned by the loss of them is alleviated by the sure and certain hope that everlasting bliss crowns their mortal labours". More worthy Sumsions! And another Michael and his wife Ann are remembered with them.

In 1774, in the list of sufferers in the fire at Colerne, Samuel Sumsion was listed as a cooper, with chattels lost to the value of £18 10s 0d, and two Michaels as publicans, losing goods to the value of £2 17s 0d and £3 0s 0d respectively.

A sad end for William Sumtion is recorded in the Wiltshire Coroners' Bills of 1752–96: "On 3rd November 1789, William Sumtion, an old man, returning home by road from North Wraxall, fell down across the stream, and unable to help himself or chilled by water". The verdict was natural death, and the Coroner received £1 13s 6d for fee and travelling expenses, eighteen miles.

In the old Marriage Register most of the marriages are between Colerne couples, but in 1812 Charlotte Sumsion was married to William Bourne of Cripplegate, London. The answer to this intriguing wedding might be that twelve years previously Florence Sumsion had married George Bourne of Melksham. Is it too much to hope that Aunt Florence Bourne was a matchmaker!

George Bourne of Melksham appears again in the will of Ann Sumsion, widow, dated October 1808 in which she left £5 to her son Michael and her watch to her daughter Ann Blatchley Sumsion. All the rest of her estate was left in trust to Mr George Bourne of Melksham and Mr Samuel Hallett to be invested and the interest paid to her daughters. She says more than once in the will that the daughters only shall benefit, and the will ends: "and my meaning is that the interest left by this my Will to my daughters shall not in any case be demanded or used by their husbands in their lifetime, but paid only to them or for their use". She was certainly a believer in Women's Rights!

Another interesting will, dated 1833 is that of Michael Sumsion, Gentleman of Colerne, who must have owned quite a lot of property. In 1816, in a transaction buying a farmhouse and land in Colerne, he had described himself as a brewer, so he seems to have gone up in the world by the time he made his will! His brewery may have been the one that stood in the garden of Elmsleigh in the Market Place, which proved a failure from lack of water, and was subsequently known as 'Sumsion's Folly'. His will, dated 2nd January 1833, and sealed with a large seal MS, left his freehold estates in Colerne, Marshfield, Box and Corsham, to William Beard Newman of Corsham, Gentleman, and Ambrose Emmerson of Batheaston, Miller, all in trust and to be sold. The interest on the capital was to provide "one clear annuity or annual sum of £150 for my dear wife Frances, as long as she remains a widow and unmarried"; the remainder of the interest from stocks, funds and securities, was to be divided between his children in equal shares for and towards their maintenance and education. The two gentlemen were also made executors and guardians of the children. But in January 1837, four years later, they both renounced their trusts. Mr Newman was then living in Manchester, Jamaica, and the legal document of renunciation was signed there. The Archdeacon of Wiltshire took over all the many legal transactions, and Frances, the widow, was made executrix in June of the same year. She must have been an exceptional woman to have been given the responsibility in those days.

In the 1841 census there are many Sumsions in the village. Frances, a keeping farmer at Euridge, with a bailiff and two servants; a mason, a cooper, agricultural labourers, and three thatchers, two of them being John Sumsions. Twenty years later, in the 1861 census, there are still Sumsion agricultural labourers, also Elizabeth Sumsion, a widow, living in Totts Lane, is recorded as a monthly nurse. By this time, one of the thatchers called John Sumsion in the 1841 census, had a son John, aged 16, who was also a thatcher. It is possible that this son John was the first village lamplighter in 1896, employed by the Parish Council to attend to the lighting, extinguishing and servicing of the lamps, including the supplying of lamp oil. For all of this he was paid 6s 0d a week.

Thatching went on as an occupation in the family, as in 1927 Maurice Sumsion won prizes at the Bath and West and Southern Counties Show held in Bath.

There are also Sumsions from Colerne in Utah, U.S.A., descended from Daniel who was born in Colerne in 1810, son of Daniel and Jane Sumsion. He married Ellen Spender from Bradford on Avon in 1837 and went to London with his wife, where his son William was born the next year. They were baptised into the Mormon Church in 1842, and returned to Colerne where their son George was born. After five years Daniel and Ellen, with their two sons left England for America and the Mormon State of Utah. William, their eldest son, became a railroad contractor and farmer, and lived in Springville, Utah, for 77 years,

Fig 27 Mr and Mrs John Sumsion

Fig 28   Mr Maurice Sumsion cutting 'spicks' and demonstrating thatching

SOMERSET RURAL COMMUNITY COUNCIL

RURAL INDUSTRIES
EXHIBITION   *&*   *&*

Certificate of Merit

Name _____ *M. C. Sumsion* _____

𝕏𝕏𝕏𝕏𝕏𝕏𝕏𝕏𝕏

BATH & WEST & SOUTHERN COUNTIES SHOW
BATH   *&*   1927

Fig 29

had two wives and 19 children, the eleventh of whom was Jesse, whose descendants have formed a Sumsion Association and correspond regularly with each other. One of them called on Mrs James Beer (née Sumsion) in Silver Street, and corresponded with her over a number of years.

The Tanners

The first Tanner appearing in the old Marriage Register is in 1662: "Benjamin, son of Alice Tanner of Colerne, widow, being a carpenter, and Sarah Webb of Colerne, spinster, married at Ditcheridge".

The Widow Tanner appears quite a few times in "The Progress of Warden Woodward", the Warden of New College in the late 1600s, who went round New College properties in Colerne inspecting trees and the houses of the College tenants to make sure they were being kept in good repair, and also to settle disputes. He had a bailiff, Mr Harris, who lived in Colerne and who carried out the Warden's instructions. In September 1663, Mr Harris was to tell Widow Tanner of "the leaneing of her house in Colerne" with the threat of forfeiture if it was not mended. In May 1666, it is recorded that the house was not mended, but wood had been assigned to her for repair. In the same year she is in trouble for allowing her cattle to trespass, but a year later the cattle are no longer trespassing. In July 1671, Benjamin Tanner confessed to having cut down two trees without permission, and a writ was ordered to be served on the family for trespassing on College woods. The record continues:

> On the morrow, being Tuesday in the morneing, the widdow and her two sonnes came to the farme to compound with us. I asked them 20s viz. 10s for the timber and 10s for the trespasse, which at last the younger brother, rather than to be served with a writ, did lay downe. But upon entreaty returned unto him 5s and at last with much difficultie 5s more by Mr. Harris, soe that all that was paid was only 10s. After this, the widdow and the sonne that lives with her, desired some timber from off the premises to mend their house. I granted also and signed a warrent for that, allowing for the present noe more than was necessarie, the rest, God willing, may be allowed at our next coming.

They must have returned home happier than when they set out!

The family seem to have continued in woodcraft, as in 1704, another Benjamin Tanner, carpenter, was married to Jone Veare, and in the 1841 census there are five carpenters in Colerne named Tanner.

They were also farmers, and in the fire in Colerne (1774), John Tanner, a farmer, lost chattels to the value of £215, the second highest amount stated in the list of sufferers. In the 1841 census, Francis Tanner had a farm, with his wife Florida, and son Giles, a carpenter, and in the first local directory of 1848 Edward Tanner was at Smiths Farm, below Ogbourne, and Awdrey Tanner at Crooks Farm, towards Thickwood. By 1851 Giles, the carpenter, had become a master carpenter, and had moved to the High Street with his wife Martha, and had an Excise Officer as a lodger. Ten years later, Giles had taken over Smiths Farm of 40 acres, and employed a man and a boy. No doubt his children, Albert, Francis, Henryetta, Sarah and Awbrey, all helped on the farm when they were not at school, and Martha, their mother, must have been very busy looking after them all!

In the local directories of the late 1800s, there were Tanner farmers, carpenters, wheelwrights and shopkeepers in the village, and William Tanner kept the Fox and Hounds Inn in 1885. In 1875 Henry Tanner was a shopkeeper and wheelwright until 1899, and in 1903 another William Tanner is recorded as a wheelwright and carpenter for the next ten years.

In 1913 Ernest Tanner was a general dealer and kept the Jubilee Provision Stores in the High Street, opposite Silver Street – the name can still be seen on the building – and John Tanner had a butcher's shop, and both kept going until at least 1926.

In the 1920s Jack Tanner lived in Ogbourne and did various jobs in the village. One of these was to stun the pigs the villagers brought to him before they were killed. Nearly everyone kept a pig or two in their garden and the saying was "if you had a pig in the sty you could always pay the rent". People in the village now can remember, as schoolboys, the excitement when the word went round that Jack Tanner was going to kill a pig. He would call out to the onlookers "Stand back lads", and swing his stunner with deadly aim. He was also Chief of the local fire brigade.

The Tanners owned houses in the High Street, and in the garden of No. 32, where Mrs Tanner still lives, there is said to be a saw-pit, a reminder of the many Tanner carpenters who lived in the village.

In the churchyard there is a multiple memorial on a tombstone to some of the Tanner family. It is dated 1897 in memory of Charles Tanner, and is inscribed

In this churchyard also repose the remains of several generations of his ancestors, his father and mother, sisters and brothers, Aubrey, George and William, Mary and Jane. His brothers Edmond and Charles are buried elsewhere. "And with the morn those angel faces smile, which we have loved long since and lost awhile".

The Tileys

The name Tiley means tiller of the soil, husbandman or farmer, and down the generations the Tiley families have lived up to their name. In the census of 1841, there were fifteen Tileys in Colerne working on the land, a farmer, hurdlemaker, woodmen and agricultural labourers.

The earliest record of the name is John Tilley, who was reported to the Exchequer in 1613 for charging excessive interest on a six month loan of £300 made by him and William Salmon, both of Colerne. This may be the same John who put up the memorial on the north wall of the church to his wife Elizabeth, who died in 1627. If it is, he must have been a man of some substance, both to make such a large loan and to put up the memorial, which reads:

> As nature paide the debt to death
> Which Adam firste did merit
> So doth my soule by Christ His
> Death eternal life inherit
> I dye not but doe change my life frede
> Now from woes from cares from strif
> No soner borne but we begin to dye
> For in this grave my house of rest I
> Lye my soule to heaven with angels fly
> For I believe that Christ for me did dye.

Memento Mori
Here lyeth the bodye of Elizabeth late wife of John Teyly who decesed the 20th day of July in the yeare of our Lord Anno Dom 1627

The earliest recorded marriage is in 1674: Joshop Tily married Ane Lediat on 29th September. In 1677, John Tily and Joane Chyvers were married on 30th September, and in 1712 John received 1s 0d for "Mending bounds at Doncom" according to the accounts in the Church Register. It is possible that this Joane Tily, is the same Joane, a widow, whose will is dated 1732. She had seven sons, six of whom, John, Richard, Thomas, Jeames, Joseph and Peter, were to receive one shilling apiece "one month after my decease" – cut off with a shilling! – but to her loving son William, who was to be her executor, she bequeathed "all the rest and residue of my personal goods and whatsoever". What a story lies behind this! Her loving son William did not inherit a great deal: the "Inventory of all the goods of Jone Tily of the Parish of Collern, widow, deceased, taken the 28th day of Febary in the year of our Lord 1734" (two years after her will) reads as follows:

	£	s	d
Imprimis The waring Aparoll	02	00	00

Item In the kichon
    One tabelbord and form, 5 small
    kitels, two pots, one Chespres [cheesepress]

with other lumber	01	15	00

    One Barel three dishes of pewter,

two bowls	00	06	06

    In the Chamber
    Two beds and bedsteds, blankets
    and coverleds, and all the Apertances
    thereunto belonging, two quasons [cushions]

and box with some lumber	03	00	00
in mony	09	00	00

Appraised by us
Thomas Edwards   William Phelps
Attested at Chippenham by the Notary Public, 10th July 1735.

Towards the middle of the 1800s some of the Tileys were maltsters and landlords of public houses in the village. In 1840, Henry Woodham Tiley, licensed victualler, signed a will leaving everything to his "dear wife Hannah", and in 1848 James Tyley was landlord and maltster at the Old Fox and Hounds till at least 1855, and William Tylee kept the White Hart in Colerne. In the 1861 census among the fourteen households of Tileys, a widow, Susan Tiley, aged 70, is down as a "Parish Messenger". Was she an early postwoman? In the same year, Elijah Tiley, a hurdlemaker, was living in the High Street, with his wife and four children, and James Tiley was a brewer lodging in Mortimers with James Jones, the schoolmaster and Parish Clerk, with his wife Anne who was a dressmaker; the eldest of their six children, Anne, is recorded as being deaf. It was probably their son James who was elected to the first Parish Council in 1894.

In the early 1900s Henry Tiley was a keen bellringer. He worked for Irelands, lived in a caravan, and wherever he was he would walk home to Colerne on a Saturday night so that he could ring the church bells on Sunday. His father, Elijah, had paid one penny a week for his schooling.

Fig 30   Mr James Tiley mowing

Fig 31   John Tiley outside Watersnaps Cottage

On the village war memorial in the Market Place, William and Alfred Tiley's names are inscribed as having given their lives in the 1914–18 war, and in the 1939–45 war, Sq. Leader William Tiley MBE was among those from the village who died.

One of the Tiley families in the 1861 census, living in Tutton Hill, had the youngest 'tiller of the soil' on record: Alfred, aged 10, was listed as a ploughboy! There are still Tileys in Tutton Hill today: Albert Tiley carries on the tradition of working with the soil. He is an expert gardener, and has won many prizes for his allotment in Bath Road. And there are other Tileys in the village: Mrs Winifred Tiley has lived in her cottage for 56 years in Silver Street, formerly called Totts Lane, where so many of the old Tiley families lived. Although she is housebound she always has had a 'garden' of pot plants in her sitting-room window.

Agriculture, Industry and Trade before 1900

Adrian Wood

Introduction

All settlers require basic essentials. These include water, materials with which to build adequate shelter and cultivable land. Until relatively recent times a prospective settlement had also to be in a location which could easily be defended. From Iron Age through Roman times the area around Colerne provided those essentials and it is probable that settlements have prospered here for at least two thousand years.

Excavations at Bury Wood Camp, an Iron Age hill fort in the north of the parish, have revealed that agriculture and animal husbandry were already developed by about 200 BC. Quernstones, used for grinding corn by hand, have been turned up by the plough in fields close to, and within the boundaries of the camp. Animal bones found there have included those from sheep, pigs, cattle and horses. It appears that weaving was carried on, as a bone bobbin and fragments of a pottery loom weight have been unearthed on the site. Although the site of one Roman villa is well known, a scattering of artifacts of suspected Roman origin, in fields between Colerne Park and Colerne Down, suggests that cultivations were not restricted to the immediate surroundings of the villa. It may be that the villa was not the only human habitation in the Colerne area in Roman or Romano-British times. With the Romans, of course, came the roads and these provided a basis for movement of goods and people, reinforcing the network of prehistoric tracks.

There is no direct evidence of continued settlement in the area until late Anglo-Saxon times but it seems hardly likely that the area would have been entirely abandoned, as those features which had attracted the earliest settlers were still there to be exploited. Entries for Colerne and Thickwood in Domesday Book show quite clearly that there was cultivated land in the two Manors, and a watermill which at that time would have been a corn mill. Land was already being ploughed and until the mid-thirteenth century oxen were used for drawing the ploughs. Only the relatively level ground would have been put to the plough, leaving the steeper slopes for woodland or, where it had been cleared of trees, for cattle or sheep to graze. The importance of oxen and sheep is curiously intertwined in the record of a trial in the year 1276. Christine le Oxehurde pleaded guilty to taking two sheep at Colerne and was sentenced by the Justices to be hanged. The Justices in the case were Sir William de Braybuf and Sir Hereward of the Marsh.

Woodland played an important part in the local economy, for it is recorded that the sale of timber from some manorial woodlands, including those in Colerne, was an important source of revenue for the Lords of the Manors.

Medieval development

William of Colerne, Abbot of Malmesbury (1260–96), had lands and property in Colerne which eventually passed to what is now New College, Oxford. He was Abbot at a time when agriculture was expanding in Wiltshire and he is known to have been an enthusiastic champion of agricultural development. He had large building programmes for his farms and was active in bringing more and more land under cultivation. At the time of his death the enclosure of open farmland was being started, and by 1311 Colerne Park had been created. This, in itself, effectively removed 200 acres from the pool of open or common land in the parish.

Colerne, Thickwood and Euridge Manors were all under the Barony of Castle Combe. The population at that time depended on the land for sustenance and livelihood. They were subject, however, to the dictates of the Lords of the Manors and few of the latter looked on the manorial lands as anything other than a source of revenue. Apart from the sale of timber, the economy depended to a great extent on rearing sheep, removing the wool and weaving and dyeing cloth which could be sold at a profit. The manors which were held under the Barony of Castle Combe were operated in an integrated system of enterprise during the early fourteenth century. Yearling sheep were sent to Colerne and Stert on an annual basis from the manor of Heytesbury which was the breeding centre. Some years later it became the practice to return older sheep to Heytesbury in order to maintain the flock there. Fleeces from Colerne, together with those from other manors, were collected centrally, again at Heytesbury.

Throughout the fourteenth century water power was exploited on an increasingly intensive basis as many fulling mills were constructed. (Fulling is the process of cleaning and thickening cloth using fuller's earth and water and beating the cloth with wooden hammers called 'stocks'. When the cloth had been fulled it was hung outside on wooden frames called 'racks', to dry.) Castle Combe was rapidly becoming an important centre for cloth under Sir John Fastolf (who became Lord of the Manor through marriage in 1409). It is probable that Colerne would have been affected by this local upsurge in the cloth industry. Certainly a comparison of taxes for 1344 indicates that Colerne was the most prosperous village locally, superior even to Castle Combe. In 1377 tax returns show a similar situation. As early as the late thirteenth century cloth manufacture and finishing must have been well established in Colerne, for the records of Malmesbury Abbey rentals reveal that rents were being received from two weavers and a dyer in the parish. It was then a common practice for farmers' womenfolk to occupy much of their time in spinning and carding wool and it is likely that such work was going on in Colerne.

Direct references to fulling and dyeing cloth at Colerne are scarce prior to the seventeenth century. Nevertheless it can be surmised that Colerne would have developed on similar lines to Castle Combe.

Rise and decline of the watermills

Watermills were being built, extended and adapted along the length of the By Brook and its tributary, the Broadmead Brook. By the time the local woollen industry had peaked, in the late eighteenth century, there appear to have been about twenty five watermills operating between the source and the confluence with the Avon at Batheaston.

The earlier mills had only been used for grinding corn, some being seasonal mills which could only work during periods of relatively high water flow. Others would have made use of small mill ponds (as at Doncombe Mill), where sufficient water could be stored to sustain the mill for longer periods, especially when water levels were unusually low. The fulling mills needed more power for longer periods and throughout every working day.

It became common practice on the By Brook (as it was elsewhere) to construct long straight leats upstream of the mills. The leats might be wide or deep depending on the situation at each mill and would have to be designed to hold sufficient water for a full day's working. Fortunately the By Brook is spring fed throughout its length and there would be few occasions when one mill would rob another of an adequate water supply. Hatches would be closed at the mills each night and the natural flow would pass into the mill head or leat and only overflow when the leat was full to capacity. In some areas of the country this led to bitter and sometimes violent disputes between mill owners. One can well imagine the feelings of a miller waking to find that he had no water because a mill upstream had stored all the previous night's flow. The result would be that there was no overflow from which the downstream mill could benefit. There do not appear to have been any such disputes on the By Brook despite the number of mills along its length. Probably the flow was adequate for everyone's needs.

In this area, the scale and variety of the necessary water engineering works are still apparent. Walking from Ford, in the downstream direction, the public footpath crosses the By Brook at Grid Ref ST838745. On the further side of the bridge the controls of a sluice can still be seen. They have been redundant for many years but at one time this sluice controlled the flow into an extremely long leat which fed the upper of two watermills at Slaughterford. The whole of the leat has been filled in but the careful observer can still find two bridges, almost buried, which gave access between fields on either side of the leat. This long leat is shown quite clearly on the Ordnance Survey 1:25000 map ST87 still being sold up to about 1985.

The developers of Chapps Mill in Colerne parish were faced with a more difficult problem. Their site was too close to the Slaughterford

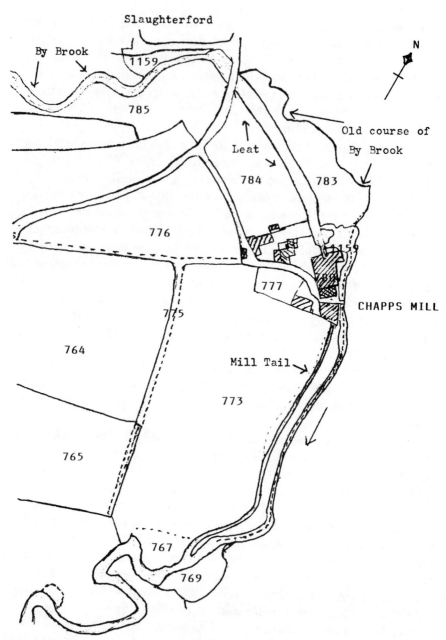

Fig 32   Chapps Mill leat and tail

Fig 33   Chapps Mill leat (the old course of the By Brook runs along the foot of the hill in the background)

(Rag Mill) site to enable a long leat to be excavated. Instead, they cut a wide new channel direct to the mill from the bridge then diverted the whole of the river into their new cut, and the original course of the river is now only discernible by a few wet patches, willows and in one or two places, a linear depression. This original course is clearly shown on the 1787 Enclosure Award map and is even now the parish boundary.

Above Widdenham Mill, where the only remaining building is the house, the By Brook again follows an unnaturally straight course for about 500 yards. This is another clear example of a man-made leat, providing the mill with extra power and a constant supply of water.

Which mill was on the site of the Domesday mill? The mill at Widdenham is much nearer to the Manor House and the village and must be the likeliest site. It is doubtful, however, that the site will ever be positively identified without a full scale archaeological excavation. What is certain is the fact that Chapps Mill and Widdenham Mill

Fig 34   Widdenham Mill site today

played important roles in the village economy through the Middle Ages and into the nineteenth century.

The earliest records of Chapps Mill refer to it as a fulling mill, leased from Wentworth Parsons of Euridge by the Drewetts, clothiers of Batheaston and Colerne. The Drewetts seem to have been established in Colerne during the seventeenth century, as the parish registers record Elizabeth Druet (surely an early variant of the name) marrying Samuel Millard in 1676. In 1687 Thomas Carington of Holt married Anne Drewett. It seems likely that male Drewetts were in the village at that time but that they were marrying women in parishes other than Colerne. The first recorded male of the family marrying locally, is Thomas Drewet (sic) who married Mrs Mary Fido on 9th September 1725. This is particularly interesting as a Thomas Drewett is on record as advertising for two pieces of drugget stolen from the racks at Chapps Mill in 1737. Thomas was succeeded by Samuel Drewett who, according to his memorial plaque in the church, died in 1791. His widow let the mill to Charles Ward (of Doncombe Mill) and William Duckett. They converted Chapps Mill to a paper mill and it was awarded Excise No. 14. The Commissioners of Customs and Excise issued lists of paper-mills and names of paper-makers together with the Excise Numbers which had been allotted.

By this time the woollen mills in the rural areas were already suffering as the work was becoming centred in towns such as Trowbridge and Bradford. A number of fulling mills on the By Brook were converted to paper-mills because they had an advantage over the towns in having the use of river water of superior quality. Peter Drewett was then living at Vale Vue House, now Vale Court. At the time of the 1787 Enclosure Award he was in occupation of what is referred to as "Peter Drewett's Dye House and Plot". According to the Enclosure map this dye house was at the southern end of Sewell Wood. Although fragments of tiles can be found in abundance there are no significant remains of a building which could have been a dye house as early as the eighteenth century. The dye house springs still rise in the area and also to be found are the dye house ponds, three small reservoirs with stone walls and the remains of control weirs. The track leading from Doncombe Lane to the ponds was called Dyehouse Lane.

We do not know whether Samuel Drewett lived at Chapps Mill. In the Enclosure Award, Chaps (sic) Mill House is recorded as being "In Demesne" of Wentworth Parsons and the occupier is not recorded. Samuel Drewett is recorded as occupying lands belonging to C P Wyndham Esq. It is of interest to note that Chapps Mill and Peter Drewett's dyehouse were both on land owned by Wentworth Parsons. Why was the dyehouse sited where it was? The site is a considerable distance from both Chapps Mill and Widdenham Mill. It was probably the fact that there was a constant supply of very high quality water at Sewell Springs which attracted the dyehouse.

On the death of Samuel Drewett's widow the lease of Chapps Mill was acquired by Robert Fowler, a Melksham wine-merchant and banker. Ward was still running the mill but in 1815 it was offered for sale as suitable for conversion to a grist or corn mill. In 1816 an Excise

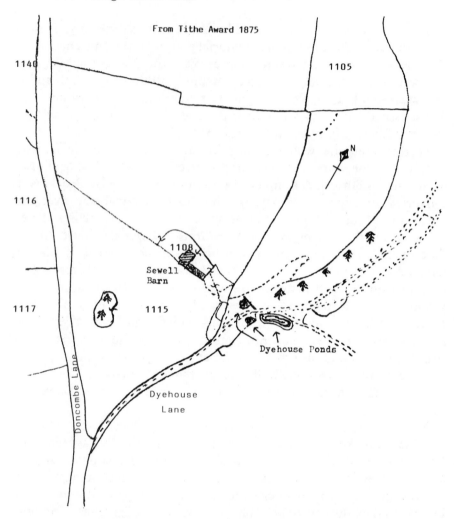

Fig 35   Peter Drewett's dyehouse ponds (note: these are sited on private land)

letter indicates that Henry Garner the younger was making paper there. In 1818 the mill had been put up for sale and William Mundy & Co of Bradford had it until about 1827. The next known owner was J W Dowding and he is listed in Kelly's Directory for Wiltshire, 1859, as being a paper manufacturer at Slaughterford.

The 1861 census for Colerne records that a man named Smith lived

Fig 36   Susanna Drewett's memorial – a reminder of the family as clothiers

at Chapps Mill cottages and that his occupation was paper-maker. Smith had moved into the parish from Calstone where, significantly, there was another paper-mill owned by Dowding. By 1871 Smith was no longer resident in the parish and Chapps Mill cottage was occupied by George Neate and his family. Neate was born in Slaughterford and his occupation was steam engine driver at the mill. So it seems that by this time the mill was no longer dependent on the river for its power and the steam engine in question may have been a stationary one used for driving the mill machinery.

Ten years later the census indicates that only William Dowding was resident at Chapps Mill, apart from a housekeeper and a domestic servant. William was aged about 35 and he was described as a "master paper manufacturer employing thirty one hands". He was also a farmer of 140 acres employing two hands. He may have been the son of the John Dowding previously mentioned. The mill is still being run as a paper-mill and is the only one remaining in the county. From the mid-nineteenth century censuses it is evident that the labour force for Chapps Mill must have been drawn from Slaughterford rather than from Colerne. Widdenham Mill might well have had a longer history than Chapps Mill but it certainly never aspired to become so important and extensive. It was a fulling mill at one time and when inspected in 1662 by a representative of New College, it was reported that the fulling stocks had fallen into disuse and that the miller had used the racks to fence his garden!

In 1787 a field near the mill was known as 'rack close' from which it is apparent that it had been the custom to dry the cloth in that particular field. Widdenham Mill was operated by Nicholas Pearce during the first half of the eighteenth century for he is recorded as having had broad white cloth stolen from the racks there in 1731. Obviously the fulling mill was then enjoying a new lease of life. Pearce mortgaged the mill in 1750 and two years later it was advertised for sale as having, "three pairs of stocks, one pair of stones and a gig mill, with a very convenient sash'd house". Pearce's son redeemed the mortgage in 1764 but by 1767 the mill was a napping mill insured for £150 and buildings on the site included a shearshop. After fulling, woollen cloth went through the process of napping. Originally this entailed tedious manual work involving the drawing of teazles across the surface of the wet cloth in order to raise the fibres. The gig was a drum, the surface of which was covered with teazles, and the cloth was drawn over the spinning drum and the nap (raised fibres) was produced mechanically. The raised fibres were of uneven length and long shears were used to trim the nap to an even finish.

A terrier (inventory of land) drawn up by New College in 1764 included land leased by Mr Anthony Drewett who then had the Manor House and Easton Town House as well as Widdenham Mill. In the 1770s Richard Hill, clothier, was carrying out dyeing at the mill for Clarks of Trowbridge. He was still at the mill in 1787. After that time the mill was converted to paper-making with Excise No. 19. The London Gazette of 12th October 1813 records that a partnership between Sarah and William Hill, paper manufacturers of Widdenham Mill, had been dissolved.

By 1841, Seth Witts, Henry Garner, Walter Garner and John Bullock were all living at Widdenham and engaged in paper-making. In Kelly's Directory for 1848 William Perren is listed as farmer and paper-maker and it appears that the four men previously mentioned worked for Perren. In 1861 John Bullock and his son were still listed as paper-makers but the mill appears to have fallen into disuse as a paper-mill shortly after this and the next record is in 1889 when John Bedford Weeks is described as a farmer and miller at Widdenham. It seems that the mill had reverted to its original role as a corn, or grist, mill.

Effects of the Industrial Revolution

For hundreds of years the economy and prosperity of Colerne was dependent on agriculture bolstered by the wool trade. With the eventual decline of rural cloth-making there was a swing to paper-making but this too failed to survive to any great extent. Industry could be sustained far better in the towns where labour was plentiful, workers' houses could be built cheaply and where access by road and rail to other parts of the country was becoming easy. Rivers were no longer a prime source of power, for the age of steam had arrived. The departure of industry must have dealt a serious blow to Colerne as well as to other villages equally remote from the industrial towns.

For a brief interval, demand for labour did increase locally while the railway was being constructed. Thousands of men were employed in tunnelling through Box Hill. Local manpower fell short of requirements and the population of nearby villages such as Colerne was inflated temporarily by railway labourers, some of whom brought their families with them. In 1841 there was a total of 66 labourers in lodgings in Colerne. Six of these, together with a boy of twelve (also a railway labourer), were living at the White Hart in the Market Place. Edwin Sheppard was a family man and he was staying with his wife Jane and two year old son at the house of James Gibbons, a grocer in the High Street, with Elias Tuckey, the smith.

Stone quarrying

Once Brunel's tunnel had been completed the population of Colerne stabilised and varied little for the next fifty years. The minimum was in 1861 at 1040 and the maximum was in 1871 at 1096. With the decline of traditional local industries, a boom in stone quarrying must have been welcomed. Box tunnel was the trigger for this boom. Vast reserves of high quality oolitic limestone, the famous Bath freestone, were revealed during the tunnelling. Soon afterwards a number of men from Colerne found work in the stone quarries around and under Box Hill.

Nearer to home, quarries had been worked for centuries. A large quarry had been developed immediately to the north of the Manor House. Most of the buildings in the village itself would have been built using stone from that quarry. All that remains of it is a reference in the road name, Quarry Lane. Another quarry, possibly used to provide stone for building in and around Totts Lane (Silver Street), was sited about half way up that road on the east side, before the road was cut off with the coming of the airfield. Many other small quarries were opened over the years, mostly filled in long ago. These quarries were a source of stone for road-making and for stone-walling. Often they provided stone for buildings erected close by. A house builder would select a site for his house and would then dig out the stone as near as possible so that the stone needed to be carried the minimum distance. This was particularly true of the more remote buildings in the parish. There was, for instance, a quarry close to the complex of buildings at Euridge and there was another close to Widdenham. There was also a large quarry between Bury Wood Camp and Mount Scylla farm.

The smaller quarries were probably worked by farm labourers and the stone used directly by a builder or mason. Only the larger quarries would have been worked by full-time quarrymen. A second large quarry was opened in Lucknam Park. It is claimed that all of the buildings at Lucknam were constructed with stone from that quarry. It seems likely that the Lucknam quarry would also have furnished stone for Sewell Barn, Northwood Farm, Peter Drewett's dyehouse and the walling round the dyehouse ponds. Stone here would have been cut directly from the steep hillside, resulting in a vertical quarry face. This type of working may have been all that was required to produce enough stone for the original buildings.

Fig 37   Lucknam quarry in the nineteenth century

There was an increased demand for stone for construction of walls round the newly enclosed fields after the Enclosure Acts of the eighteenth and nineteenth centuries. A look around the parish shows that walls have consumed vast quantities of stone. In addition to the enclosures, roads, both public and private, were defined and a great deal of broken stone would have been used in road making at that time. Some of the walling stone could well have been found on the surface of the ground, especially where it had been ploughed. Most of it, though, was probably retrieved from the quarries and the quarry waste heaps. The quarry at Lucknam Park was probably reopened in the late nineteenth century when new buildings were going up and existing buildings were being extended.

It seems that the quarrymen adopted the method of caving which had been used for many years around Box. Two horizontal tunnels were cut into the base of the quarry face and a cross tunnel connected the two, some distance into the workings. The main headings were driven further into the quarry with side galleries shooting off at intervals. There is clear evidence that the underground workings are relatively recent because the stone faces left on the sides of the galleries had been sawn as opposed to having been hacked by picks. Bedding planes in the limestone at Lucknam quarry are somewhat irregular and there are many faults, fractures and fissures. The amount of waste must have been considerable and working in the quarry would not have been the safest of occupations. Extensive supports were obviously needed to avoid disastrous roof falls.

The main quarry, in the village, together with the quarry at Lucknam, must have had an impact on employment in the village. The census returns give an interesting breakdown of the numbers of men employed in the stone business. Unfortunately, though, there is no indication as to *where* the men were employed. No doubt many of them would have worked in quarries outside the parish. The crude numbers of stone workers, including quarrymen, masons, labourers and apprentices from 1841 to 1881 are as follows :-

1841	28 men	1851	23 men
1861	28 men	1871	55 men
1881	70 men		

These figures were only exceeded, as would be expected, by the number of workers in agriculture. Nevertheless the number of men employed in quarries may have been as much as twenty per cent of the male working population in 1881.

During a period approaching a thousand years the prosperity of Colerne has been maintained at a high level compared with many villages in the area. During that time a number of industries have played an important part but most of them have declined and even disappeared completely from the local scene. Such has been the case with wool and with stone. Papermaking continues in the parish, but very tenuously. Only agriculture has any real claim to survival, but even here the scene has changed dramatically. Between 1841 and 1881 the largest number of workers in agriculture was 225, in 1851. This number was made up of 36 farmers, 153 agricultural labourers, 12 shepherds, 12 ploughboys (10 to 15 year olds), and 12 hurdle-makers.

The inclusion of the last named category may well be disputed. But what of the 10 woodmen listed in the census for 1851? Maybe they should be added in. To complete this picture for that year (having already noted, above, that there were 23 men employed in the stone industry), here are the trades to which the village gave employment:

9 carpenters and an apprentice	3 maltsters and 3 labourers
1 cooper	3 smiths and an assistant
2 paper-makers and a labourer	2 saddlers
1 basketmaker	2 thatchers
1 master plasterer and an apprentice	1 tiler and plasterer
2 house decorators	1 painter
9 shoemakers	2 tailors
2 victuallers	4 bakers
1 baker and grocer	1 baker and shopkeeper
1 butcher	2 grocers
1 shopkeeper	3 carriers/carters
5 gardeners	1 policeman
1 excise officer	1 deputy surveyor
1 road labourer	8 labourers
10 dressmakers	2 seamstresses
8 laundresses	3 charwomen
2 washerwomen	

Conclusion

The nineteenth century witnessed the decline of Colerne's fortunes with only the major industry of agriculture remaining by the end of the century. The wide variety of trades listed in the censuses up to 1881 indicate that the village must then have been self supporting to a large extent.

Sadly, most of those trades and professions have now disappeared, as a check through the above list will quickly show.

Moving forward in time, from the end of the nineteenth century to the 1980s we can recall the disappearance of all but a handful of shops and those that do remain do not include a butcher or a baker. Even our local policeman is based at Corsham.

Who knows what the historians of the future will make of Colerne's economic progress through the twentieth century?

Sources

Victoria County History of Wiltshire.

Rogers K H (1976), *Wiltshire and Somerset Woollen Mills*, Pasold Research Fund Ltd.

Corfield M C (ed) (1978), *A Guide to the Industrial Archaeology of Wiltshire*, Wiltshire County Council Library and Museum Service.

Wood A A *et al* (1986), *Report of an Archaeological Project*, carried out by M.S.C. Community Programme for N.W.D.C.

Colerne Enclosure Award 1787, Wiltshire Record Office, Trowbridge.

Colerne Tithe Award 1875, Wiltshire Record Office, Trowbridge.

A Caring Community

Poverty and Poor Laws in Colerne up to 1834

Joyce and John Utting

Introduction

Despite recent controversy about the definition of poverty, the social historian is compelled to accept that there is no absolute standard. Clearly, those whom we consider 'poor' in Britain today would have appeared immeasurably rich in the Middle Ages, or even to most of the population of Africa and Asia now. It follows that in looking at poverty in a historical context we have to accept the standards of the time. The 'poor' are those who were generally considered poor at the time.

In earliest times in England very few people would have been considered poor: just those who were unable to work through age or other infirmity. Their needs were normally taken care of by the family or within social units such as the Iron Age fort and Roman villa in Colerne. Later the Manors largely took care of their own elderly, widows, sick and infirm, and the Church also accepted a moral responsibility for alms-giving and the care of the sick. But in the fourteenth and fifteenth centuries, as towns developed and the manorial system broke down, the burden on the Church increased; and the dissolution of the monasteries by Henry VIII meant that it could no longer cope.

The State was forced to intervene. At first its action was purely punitive, but this proved ineffective and during the second half of the sixteenth century a more comprehensive system of poor relief was developed. In 1572 the first compulsory poor rate was ordered. Eventually, the great Poor Law of 1601 was enacted, and this remained the basis for official action to relieve poverty for more than two hundred years.

The guiding principle of the 1601 Poor Law was that each parish was to be responsible for its own poor. The able-bodied were to be put to work; the 'impotent poor' (who could not work) would be relieved; children could be apprenticed; and vagrants and those who refused work could be punished and made to work in 'houses of correction'. Each parish was to appoint 'Overseers of the Poor' to carry out these responsibilities and their endeavours were to be financed by a poor rate, levied on householders in the parish. This system, with various amendments, continued until 1834, when a new Poor Law replaced the parish overseers with Boards of Guardians, with responsibility for 'unions' of parishes, and this continued until 1930.

The surviving records of parish administration of the Poor Laws in Colerne are the account books of the Overseers of the Poor (three volumes, covering the periods 1688–1742, 1805–18 and 1819–32) and, to a much lesser extent the churchwardens' account book for 1755–1868. The last of these overseers' accounts takes us almost up to the enactment of the Poor Law of 1834. After that, the relief of poverty in Colerne was part of the responsibilities of the Chippenham Guardians of the Poor, who held their first meeting on 3rd December 1835. Some idea of the ways in which their operations affected the village may be obtained from their minute books; the first two volumes, each of some 360 hand-written pages, cover the period up to 28th September 1838; then, after a short gap, there is an unbroken sequence from 11th July 1845 until 1930.

In this account we have concentrated on the truly local administration by the parish overseers, trying to show how they interpreted and operated the national legislation of 1601 and the subsidiary Acts up to 1834; the changes after 1834 must, for the most part, await further study.

The years 1688–1742

The first year for which we have overseers' accounts, 1688, was the year in which William and Mary came to the throne. The Poor Law of 1601 had been in force for nearly a century; but in Colerne the relief of the poor was clearly quite a minor problem. The accounts at this time are fairly bare, with only sparse details, but it appears that throughout the period 1688–1742 the number of people receiving regular help from the parish was usually less than ten and never more than thirteen. In 1688 itself there were seven regular recipients and their total receipts for the year were £33 13s 6d – an average of rather less than 2s 0d a week each.

These regular payments would have been made to poor people who were considered unable to work to keep themselves and who had no other means of support: mainly widows, the sick and the elderly. They were made every four weeks during the year for which the overseers served, which began on Lady Day (25th March) so that the 'year 1688' was actually 1688–89.

Besides these regular payments the overseers also paid what their accounts call "extraordinary expenses". These cover the cost of any help given in kind (e.g. clothing) as well as payments made to anybody who was not one of their regular clients and their own expenses in doing the job. It is the details of these payments, when they are given, which provide a flavour of the way the overseers saw their job and the spirit in which it was undertaken. In 1688 these extraordinary expenses, at £19 14s 4d came to more than half as much as the regular payments, so they represent a significant part of the overseers' work. They made the total expenditure for that year up to £53 7s 10d. In 1741–2, the last year in this account book, the total was £109 0s 7d for fourteen 'months' of four weeks each.

The early nineteenth century

After 1742 there is a gap in the available overseers' accounts for Colerne until 1805, the year of the battle of Trafalgar, and we then have an unbroken sequence until 1832. Churchwardens' accounts, from 1755, mention payments made by them but these are only to people (mainly soldiers and sailors) passing through the village. The amounts are usually 6d or sometimes 1s 0d for several people together or on one occasion in 1758 "to a man lost by Fyer". These payments by the churchwardens are few, and even fewer after about 1760; but casual payments of a similar kind can still be found in the overseers' records from 1805.

By this time the relief of the Colerne poor had been quite transformed, by comparison with the early eighteenth century. This is reflected not only in the numbers of people relieved and the cost to the parish, but also in the care taken in the presentation of the accounts and the amount of detail shown in them. The standard form was now a detailed list (by name of the recipient) of all the regular payments for each four-weekly period, together with an annual list of all the extraordinary payments with a statement of the purpose of each.

The number of regular payments had risen to some fifty, ranging from 4s 0d to 18s 0d each and totalling about £25 per 'month'. These grew fairly steadily over the next 25 years to about sixty recipients, totalling about £32 a month in the early 1830s. The extraordinary payments fluctuated more widely, but in most years they continued to amount to some 50–60 per cent of the regular allowances, making total payments in 1830–31, for instance, of £674.

The most important thing about this great increase is that it was due to an increase in numbers rather than the amount of the individual allowances. As noted in Roger Clifton's contribution, there was no great change in prices, such as we should expect today, during the eighteenth century and this is reflected in the fact that the average allowance increased only from about 7s 6d per month in 1700 to about 10s 0d per month in the 1800s. But the number of people receiving regular payments had grown five- or six-fold in the same period.

Unfortunately, the gap in the available overseers' accounts prevents us from pin-pointing any particular period in the later eighteenth century as the time when this increase occurred, but we do know that there was a general increase in poverty during this time and Colerne was not unique. It has been suggested (see "The Village Labourer" by J L and Barbara Hammond, for instance) that the enclosures were an important cause of rural poverty, because they deprived all but the larger farmers of their common and other rights which had enabled them to keep cows to contribute to their sustenance. The main enclosures in Colerne took place as a result of the Act of 1787, well within the period when we know the increase occurred, although we have no actual records of poor relief at that time.

That the fifty or so regular recipients of help were only the poorest of the poor seems to be implied by a special Memorandum inserted in the accounts for 1807 which states:

George Tuckey residing in the Parish of Colerne was Convicted before Thomas Bruges Esq One of his Majesty's Justices of the Peace for the said County, for having Snares found in his House for the destroying Game, and paid a fine of Five pounds. One moiety [half] whereof was given in Bread to the Poor of the said Parish.

There follows a list of no less than 92 names each receiving bread to the value of either 4¾d or 9½d with a total of £2 3s 11¼d. The sum of 9½d appears to have been the price of a 'gallon' of bread (equivalent to 8lbs, or rather more than four of today's large loaves).

The Overseers of the Poor

The office of overseer was actually created in 1572; it was formalised by an Act of 1597–8, which provided for their appointment by the Justices, and confirmed by the Poor Law of 1601. This ordered the churchwardens and two to four other substantial householders to be nominated each year as overseers of the poor, with the duty of putting the able-bodied poor to work and providing maintenance for those who were unable to work.

Overseers were nominated by the Parish Vestry, a meeting open to all parishioners which was held annually at about Easter and at other times as needed. It was both a 'civil' and a 'church' meeting, combining the functions of the present Parish Council and the annual Church Meeting (the part of the latter when churchwardens are elected is still called a Vestry Meeting). The appointment of overseers had to be ratified by the Justices and this, like other things requiring their approval entailed the payment of a fee and the expense of a journey, amounting to a few shillings.

In many of the years covered by our records just two overseers were appointed, but even when there were more, only two of them usually acted. Their methods of working depended on the individuals concerned; sometimes they seem each to have taken responsibility for alternate months, sometimes for several consecutive months up to a full half-year, and sometimes – particularly in the later years – joint responsibility for the whole year. The form and detail of their accounts also depend very much on the individual although, as a general rule, the amount of detail is sparse in the earlier records and

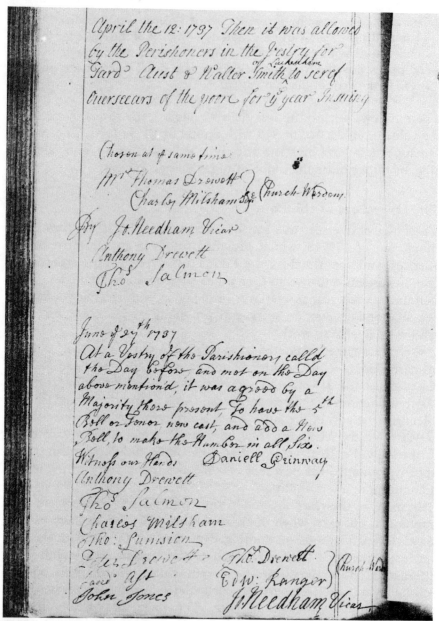

Fig 38   Appointment of overseers, 1737 (at foot, decision to add fifth and sixth church bells)

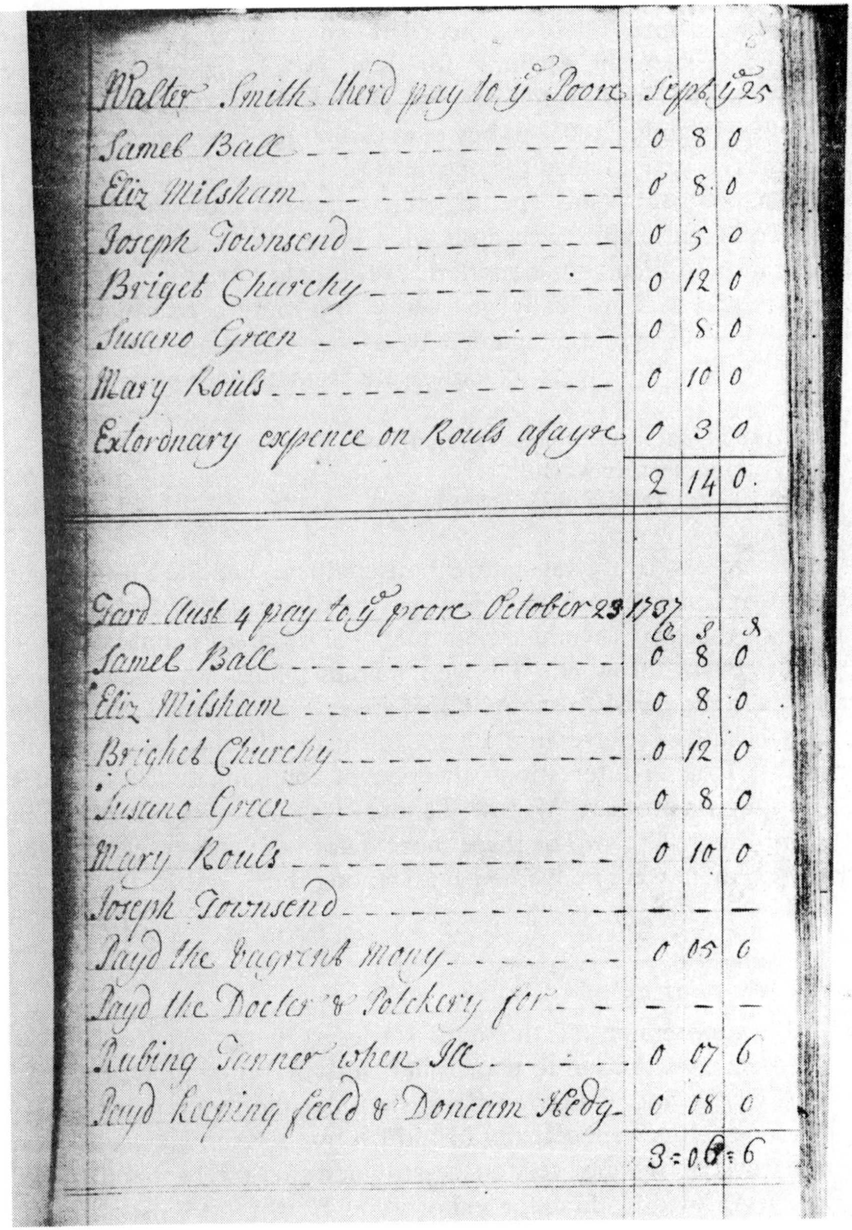

Walter Smith third pay to ÿ Poore Sept ÿ 25

	£	s	d
Samel Ball _ _ _ _ _ _ _ _ _ _ _ _	0	8	0
Eliz Milsham _ _ _ _ _ _ _ _ _ _	0	8	0
Joseph Townsend _ _ _ _ _ _ _ _	0	5	0
Briget Churchy _ _ _ _ _ _ _ _	0	12	0
Susano Green _ _ _ _ _ _ _ _	0	8	0
Mary Rouls _ _ _ _ _ _ _ _ _ _	0	10	0
Extrordnary expence on Rouls afayre	0	3	0
	2	14	0

Gard Aust 4 pay to ÿ poore October 23 1737

	£	s	d
Samel Ball _ _ _ _ _ _ _ _ _ _	0	8	0
Eliz Milsham _ _ _ _ _ _ _ _ _	0	8	0
Brighet Churchy _ _ _ _ _ _ _	0	12	0
Susano Green _ _ _ _ _ _ _ _	0	8	0
Mary Rouls _ _ _ _ _ _ _ _	0	10	0
Joseph Townsend _ _ _ _ _ _	—	—	—
Payd the vagrent mony _ _ _ _ _ _	0	05	0
Payd the Docter & Potckery for _ _	—	—	—
Rubing Tanner when Ill _ _ _ _ _	0	07	6
Payd keeping feeld & Doncam Hedg	0	18	0
	3	06	6

Fig 39   Page from overseers' accounts, 1737

increases with time. There is a record of two occasions when they paid somebody to keep the accounts for them: in 1723 there is an entry "Paid Charles Hamilton for keeping of ye book, ye rate and Indentures: 12s 0d" and in 1805–6 they paid Collatinus Rawlings the sum of five guineas a year to keep the accounts.

The handwriting and spelling too are very individual! In the seventeenth century the writing is what is known as 'secretary hand', which can be difficult for a modern eye to read (an example appears in fig 41) and this gradually gives way to a more copperplate style, which is not always accompanied by a corresponding improvement in spelling. The following examples are from the accounts of 1737:

Payd the Doctor and Potckery [apothecary]	
for Rubing Tanner when ill	7s 6d
Payd keeping feeld and Doncam Hedg	8s 0d

The overseers, being substantial householders, include a number of well known Colerne surnames. Besides the four families discussed by Joan Platt, there are several appointments of different people with the surnames Brokenbrow and Drewett, names which have now disappeared from the parish, although there are several examples among the memorials and, of course, in the name of the mill just across the parish boundary. It is an interesting reflection of changing social attitudes that although a woman (Widow Tanner) was appointed overseer in 1709 and there were two or three more before the gap in our records after 1742, there were no women at all among the overseers from 1805 to 1832.

Paying for poor relief

After the suppression of the monasteries it became necessary to replace their contribution to poor relief, and an Act of 1536 provided that the clergy and churchwardens should collect voluntary alms. Other private alms were actually forbidden by this Act. However, this voluntary system was not very successful, and there were soon further enactments providing first for exhortation by the bishops, then by magistrates and eventually, if persuasion failed, for compulsion by the magistrates. Finally, in 1572, a compulsory levy was authorised, thus bringing into existence the system of 'rates' based on the annual value of property, which survived for more than 400 years.

Colerne records include rating lists for 1721, 1735 and 1787. The oldest of these, headed "A Single Rate for ye Poor made in 1721" shows the amount raised by a rate of 1d in the £. It lists 105 (presumably distinct) properties, although there are many cases where several belong to the same person; the number of owners is only 69, of whom nine are women, mainly described as wid[ow]. Three intriguing entries, which do not seem to link up with anything elsewhere in the records, relate to Daniel Greenway, Robert Noble and Daniel Smart who are each to pay rates for "pt of ye hospitall lease" as well as another property. The two largest entries are "Sir William Hanham for ye Farm: 13s 8d" and "Dick Knight: 13s 4d", representing properties with a rateable value of about £160. Sir William Hanham had two other properties, making a total valuation of £250, not inconsiderable for those days. At the other extreme, there is one sum of ½d (but the owner had other property), two of 1½d and a number of 2d. The total product of a 1d rate is £7 14s 11¼d, equivalent to a rateable value of some £1860.

In 1787, although the rateable value is up by nearly 50 per cent to £2700, the number of entries is only 72; but there are very few cases of several properties belonging to the same person, so the number of ratepayers is little changed from 1721. Whether the reduced number of entries always results from actual consolidation of properties is not clear; that it does so to some extent would seem to be implied by the fact that the largest valuation is now £587, more than twice the amount assessed to any one person in 1721. At the bottom end there are four valuations of less than £1.

This last rating list is included in the churchwardens' accounts. The next available overseers' accounts, for 1805–32, show that there was little change in the total rateable value until 1826 when it suddenly jumped to about £4950. Since we do not have a rating list for this time we cannot be sure whether this was wholly due to revaluation or also to making more people liable to pay.

These poor rates were not levied on the basis of annual estimates of expenditure, as we have been used to in the recent past, but were charged as and when the money was needed. A rate (of so many pence in the £) was 'allowed' by a Vestry Meeting, but also had to be approved by two Justices.

In the seventeenth and early eighteenth centuries a total rate of some 7d in the £ would have been needed to finance a year's expenditure and this seems to have been levied in two or three instalments of 3d–5d a time. By the early nineteenth century the much greater expenditure (accompanied by relatively little growth in rateable value) had led to a considerable increase in the amount in the £. The standard charge at this time was 6d in the £ but a rate of this amount was collected every two or three months. No doubt the uncertainty about when a rate would be charged would have been a considerable inconvenience to the ratepayers, but there is little evidence of default or late payment in the overseers' books. Nevertheless, the growing frequency of these levies was presumably one reason for the 1826 revaluation. Without it a total charge of some 54d in the £ would have been needed in that year; in fact the actual levies were one 'old rate' at 6d in the £ and three 'new rates' each of 1s 0d in the £ of the new valuation.

Caring for the sick and elderly

One of the overseers' major concerns was the care of poor persons who were unable to work through sickness, injury or age; a duty which the Colerne overseers appear to have exercised with great care. They paid allowances, gave assistance in kind (clothing, bedding etc.) and provided for medical attention or simple home care.

The accounts do not usually state the reason for the regular monthly allowances, though we may reasonably assume that most of these were to people incapable of work; but throughout our period there are "extraordinaries" which clearly indicate help in kind or in services to the sick and elderly. Thus in 1691 extraordinary payments of £10 17s 10d included an unspecified amount for "clothes and houseroom for the poor". A few years later Richard Jones and John Holbrooke were both receiving this kind of help; here are some of the entries:

1704   July   To washing Richard Jones to Midsumer   2s 0d

	July	To Anthony Drewett's Wife For Curing John Holbrooke's Leg	5s 0d
	Aug	Given by ye parish Extraordinary to John Holbrooke	2s 6d
	Dec	For a pair of Stockings and washing Richard Jones	4s 6d
1705	Nov	Mending John Holbrooke's Bed	6s 7d
1706	Aug	Shirt for Richard Jones	3s 6d
	Sept	Blanket for Jo. Holbrooke	6s 9d
	Oct	paid bess ball for washing Rich. Jones and Jo. Holbrooke	6s 0d
	Nov	Bed mat and bedcord for Jo. Holbrooke	2s 8d
	Dec	for shooes for J. holbrooke	3s 8d

and so on for several years.

Anthony Drewett and his wife, mentioned above, apparently had some knowledge of medicine, for other entries at this time are:

1709	July	Anthony Drewett for a cure of Bess Nichols Legg	10s 0d
1714	Aug	Paid Mrs. Drewett for John Roses Cure	£1 1s 6d

These two were probably not formally qualified, but payments were also made to people described as "doctor", for example:

1711	June	Paid Dr. Polls for John Tylys Cure	£1 0s 0d
1720	Feb	Paid dr. Allinham for Comeing and things for stephen balls wife	£3 6s 10d

and a particularly expensive item:

1726	Feb	Paid Doctor Jeffery [at Box] for curing Jo. Rose	£7 7s 0d
	Dec	Paid for carrying Jo. Rose to Doctor Jefferys for man and horse	3s 6d

Another type of cure, popular at the time, is exemplified by:

1711	Oct	daniell Blathly for Bleeding Mrs and Ann [Millsam] 5 times	2s 6d
		daniel Blathly for Bleeding 3 times more	1s 6d

Childbirth also led to expenses for the overseers if the mother was poor:

1717	Apr	Jane Blatchley midwife to bess Harper	5s 0d
1736	Apr	Payd part of the Expence when ye woman lay in	10s 11½d
		Payd Dito, to the nurs hous rume etc.	£1 9s 6d

(references to "the woman" or "the man", without a name, usually imply that the person was a travelling vagrant, not settled in the parish – see also the example below).

Smallpox was a special scourge at this time and gave rise to a variety of expenses:

1718	Nov	Expenses with the man that Came from Bath about the Smallpox	1s 0d
	Dec	peter Drewett for what he Laid out att bath about the Maid in ye smallpox	£1 11s 0d
1725	Sept	Gave traviler who was with Child	3s 6d
		Gave another wooman who had the smallpox	11s 9d
1737	July	John Pointing to releeif his Famely in the smallpox	£1 9s 6d
1740	May	Payd the expence in part of Solaman Frys famely in the smallpox	£2 19s 3¾d

When sickness ended in death the overseers became involved with the funeral arrangements and expenses. The following entries from 1713 are typical:

John Sumsion for things had in walt balls sickness	2s 6d
a shroud for walt ball	3s 9d
for bread and cheese	2s 6d
for beer at burying	5s 0d
for affidavit	1s 0d
Expenses att Jane Sumpsions for walt balls sickness	3s 6d
Burying Walt Ball	4s 0d

The total funeral expenses, excluding the payments to the Sumsions, amount to 15s 0d. The bread and cheese was presumably refreshment, but "beer" (which occurs in most of these funeral accounts) should

Fig 40 Page from overseers' accounts, 1715 (includes Jos. Tyly's illness, death and funeral)

probably be spelt "bier". The affidavit would have certified that the shroud was made of wool, as required by an Act of 1667–8 which was intended for the benefit of the wool trade and was not replaced until 1814.

Another form of assistance given by the overseers was the payment of house rent. The 1691 entry already quoted refers to "house room" and in 1709 there is "Wife Fords rent: 10s 0d" but the period is not stated. However, in the following year there is a payment "John Grinaway for half a years house rent: 9s 0d", an amount which seems trivial by today's standards and still looks small even when set against some of the prices of the same period, such as those relating to J Holbrooke and R Jones above.

Fuel was also provided by the overseers. Wood was supplied to R Jones in 1708 and following years, and in 1709 there is the first mention of coal when a "sack of coal" was provided for 1s 9d. In 1712 loads of wood at 10s 0d a load were being supplied and in March 1714 Joseph Tyly received three bushels of coal costing 1s 9d and 8d worth of wood.

There is even an instance of the overseers making a loan as early as October 1713. This was £3 15s 0d to John Webb of Eastrip; the account book contains his signed pledge to repay and a note of the repayment in Sept 1714. The facts that he could sign his name and repay such a sum so quickly suggest that he was not one of the poorest.

All of the above examples are taken from the earliest volume of Colerne overseers' accounts, and show the great variety of ways in which they helped the poor and sick even before the middle of the eighteenth century. The later accounts, starting in 1805, do not show many significant changes, although there are many more items – in keeping with the increase in the number of poor people helped – and some of them are handled differently. For instance, in this later period the overseers were obviously paying an annual retainer to the doctor for routine care of the sick. The normal amount was £10 10s 0d a year; but in 1813–14 it was £11 11s 0d and there are various additional single payments, presumably either to another doctor or for some special attention. Occasional visits to the hospital also begin to appear, involving a payment of £3 0s 0d apparently for admission as an in-patient. A typical example is:

1806	Feb	Pd in Bath Ostpetle with Thos. Ford	£3 0s 0d
		Pd for halling Thos. Ford to Bath	5s 9d

Bleeding was still in fashion: there are a number of entries like "Leeches for Jane Gilman: 4s 6d" or "William Clarke for leeches 3s 0d". But a more agreeable cure is indicated by "A Bottle Port Wine for Greens Wife 6s 6d".

The usual cost of a funeral at this time was 18s 0d but one in 1807 cost £1 1s 0d "it being a Extra large Coffin for her" and a rather sad entry in 1816 records £1 10s 0d for "Sarah Eames Childrens Funerals".

Other items from 1816–18 show that the overseers were still offering help in kind in a great variety of ways, and give some idea of prices at this time (as well as some nice spellings!):

Richard Smith Smock frock and pr of Shoes	16s 0d
David Tanner Smock frock	10s 0d
Sheet and Shirt for J. Smith the elder	13s 1½d
Rebecka Ford a Blanket	7s 6d
Ann Gibbons 1lb Sugar	10½d
Pd Thacher for Ann Gibbons House	7s 2d
Paid Frances Grinway for Masons Work do.	10s 11½d
Ann Gibbons 2 Bushl Coal	2s 8d
James Smith pr of Shous	10s 6d
Cox Boy tow Surts	6s 6d
do. tow pr of Stocking	4s 4d
Dd Tanner a Shurl [shawl or shirt?]	6s 6d
Samuel Tylys Boy a pr of Breeches	2s 6d
Bed matt and Cord for A Green	5s 0d
For Making Horsmans Shirt and Smock	1s 9d
Waistcoat Breeches for Horsman	5s 6d

The last two of these entries are among a large number of payments relating to John Horsman (or Horseman); he received all kinds of clothing and bedding, was shaved from time to time (at 6d a time), and was frequently "brought" from other places, for example:

	Expences of bringing Jno Horseman from Rudloe	2s 0d
and	J. Rose for bringing in Horseman	3s 0d

It would appear that he was a simple-minded man who was given to wandering away from home; a succession of overseers showed great forbearance in bringing him back and caring for his needs.

The able-bodied poor

In principle, at least, the relief of the able-bodied poor throughout the period with which we are dealing was supposed to be achieved by putting them to work, and their readiness to do so was regarded as a test of their genuine poverty. How this was achieved is seldom clear from the overseers' accounts. It seems that in our earlier period the overseers of the poor were, in Colerne as in many other rural areas, essentially carrying out some of the functions of the surveyors of the highways. Thus in 1688 we find them paying £2 16s 2d for the repair of the bridge at Widdenham; in July 1709 they paid £1 2s 6d for the repair of the Fosse wall; and other entries for this period include:

1709	For 2 bridges	14s 2d
	For one days work stopping hedge at Donkiome	1s 0d
1710	For powder and shot and mend Doncom Geat and other things Brought	16s 2d
1711	For mending the fosse mounds to sam ball	8d
	Mending Weavin Mill Bridge	1s 0d
1712	For bridges and & 3 (sic) to the supervisors	£2 8s 11d
1714	For a gate and post at Doncom	3s 6d
	For iron belonging to the gate	1s 6d

The reference to powder and shot probably ties in with two other entries for "Keeping a Watch" and "Keeping the Fields" in 1691 and with:

1714	Richard Aust jun. for his Charge of the fields	11s 8d

An amusing item in July 1740 reads:

	Payd poore pepel to cleans the hos pool	5s 0d

The accounts are not usually so explicit but it seems likely that many entries like those above would include payment for work undertaken by the poor.

Payments of this kind are fewer in the nineteenth century accounts, although there are still some entries, e.g. in 1818–19 for "road works" or "on the road": but loss of employment and low wages were becoming so common at this time that most places were giving up any semblance of finding work for the able-bodied. Instead we often find the Colerne overseers making payments to people who are simply described as "out of employ".

Additionally, Colerne had adopted what was known as the 'Speenhamland System' or something very like it. This took its name from a meeting of the Berkshire justices at Speenhamland, near Newbury, which devised a system of making up wages to a level which was to be determined according to the size of family and the price of bread. Although it was never incorporated into the law, the system became so common that it was widely believed to have legal authority. There is no mention of the price of bread in the Colerne accounts, but the application of this type of system is clearly indicated by numerous entries for "wages made up". Presumably, the system was counterproductive in Colerne as it was elsewhere; at a time of low wages there was no incentive either to employers to pay more or to workers to seek higher wages if the parish was going to accept responsibility for making them up. This was one of the causes of the great increase in poor rates nationwide – far greater in some places than in Colerne – which led to the Poor Law of 1834.

Apprenticeships

One of the accepted ways of finding employment for pauper children, when they became old enough, was to find them apprenticeships. There are examples of this in the eighteenth century accounts:

1724	Jan	Paid att a pish meeting Mr. Samuel Ball came to take Rob Ball's boy apprentice	8s 6d
	Mar	Paid John Ball for Rob Ball's Boy and Indentures	£2 6s 0d
	July	Paid for Susan Ball's indentures	12s 0d
		Paid Henry Ball's master	£5 10s 0d

In 1729 there are more entries for Ball's boy(s), presumably younger brothers:

Jan	For having Ball's boy home	1s 0d
	In cash for Ball's Boys	£8 3s 6d
	Indentures	10s 0d

The cash was probably a payment to the Master.

In November of that same year there are entries concerning a boy (Hatherell's child) who seems to have been brought to Colerne with a removal order from elsewhere, cared for for two months, provided with hose and shoes (3s 0d) and then apprenticed for £5 10s 0d with 5s 0d for the indentures.

We have not found any such entries in the accounts for 1805–32: but apprenticeship comes up again in the records of Chippenham workhouse, though not specifically in relation to Colerne children.

Removal orders

Because each parish was responsible for its own poor and did not want to spend money unnecessarily, it was important to return outsiders to their own parishes. Indeed, prior to 1794 anybody who had not established 'settlement' in the parish (by renting a tenement worth £10 a year or more, or by being employed for more than a year, or finding security to discharge the parish from any expense on his behalf) could be returned to his own parish at any time; after that date they could only be removed if they actually became a charge to the parish.

Even when removal was a fairly simple business it would involve the overseers in some expense. Thus in January 1728 they paid out 6s 6d for "keeping of Norvell a night, Horse and hyer and Expences carrying him to Box next day" and in October the same year:

Expences when Carried Eliz Jones to Bristoll	8s 6d
For 3 men and 3 horse	10s 0d

In some disputed cases these removals could take much more time and expense. First, the pauper's settlement (his own parish) had to be established by examination before a magistrate and then a removal order had to be signed by a magistrate and the arrangements made for the actual removal. In 1813 the accounts show:

June   Jas. Rawlings Examination touching the
      Settlement of his son Jeremiah   2s 0d
      Do. for his attendance   3s 0d
      Summons for Jeremiah   2s 0d
      Expenses attending the Meeting at Chippn   5s 0d

And next month a similar set of entries includes additionally:

July 7 Jeremiah's Examination and Orders of
      removal etc   12s 0d

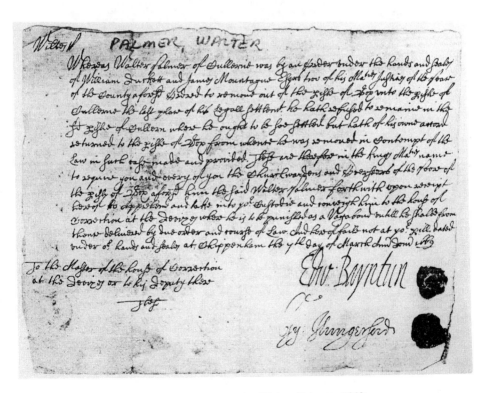

Fig 41   Removal order for Walter Palmer, 1669

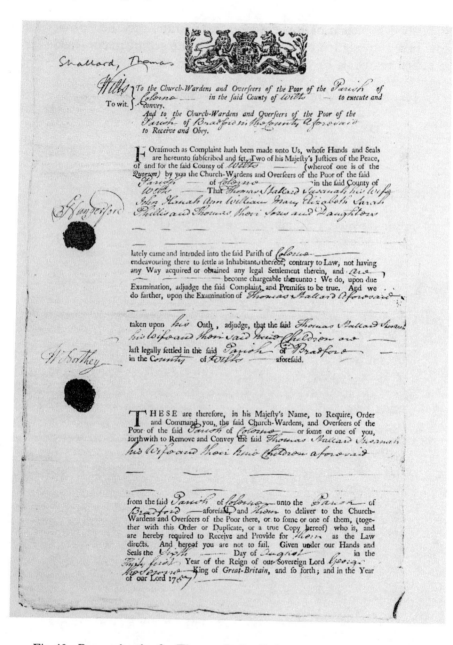

Fig 42   Removal order for Thomas Stallard's family, 1757, on standard form

Removal was so common nationally that by the middle of the eighteenth century printed forms were available with blank spaces for the insertion of local details. The Wiltshire Record Office has one such printed order, dated 1757, for the removal from Colerne to Bradford of William Stallard, his wife and *nine* children. It is easy to see why the Colerne overseers wanted to rid themselves of so great a burden! Another order in the WRO shows the punitive attitude of earlier times. This one, dated 7th March 1669 and written in longhand, orders the removal of Walter Palmer from Box to "Cullerne". Because he had disobeyed an earlier order by returning to Box after a previous removal, the overseers were instructed first to take him to "the house of correction at the Devizes where he is to be punished as a Vagabond" – which almost certainly included whipping.

Sometimes, instead of ordering removal of a pauper an arrangement was made for him to remain where he was and for the overseers of that place to receive payment for him from his own parish. An early example in the Colerne accounts occurs in 1712 when the overseers "Paid to Dimoton [Didmarton?] about Will King: £1 1s 6d": they paid 1s 1d for a "rug for King" at the same time.

A typical story from our later period starts in 1809 when Charles Isaac's landlady was about to seize his goods (presumably because he could not pay his rent):

1809	Aug	A Journey to Kingsdown to stop the Seasin of Charles Isacc Goods (By Mrs. Ladd)	2s 0d
		Given to Charles Isacc and wife being Ill at Different Times	10s 0d
	Oct	A jorney to Kingsdown to visit Charles Isacc and wife they being Ill	1s 0d
	Nov	Paid two (sic) Charles Isaac Fambley	5s 0d

and so on, until he seems finally to have been brought to Colerne in 1811 when we find:

Paid Hauling Isaack Goods to Colerne	15s 0d

We do not know the precise reason for this change but payments for Isaac's wife and rent cease around this time and there are new regular entries for "looking after Isaac: 4s 0d". Presumably his wife died and he was brought back because he was now alone and still ill.

Settlement certificates

Because the rules on settlement and removal made it so difficult for the poor to travel, even to find a job, an Act of 1696–7 authorised the issue of 'settlement certificates'. These were documents issued by the parish acknowledging that the holders had a legal settlement there and agreeing to receive them back unless they gained a settlement elsewhere. Obviously these documents were valuable both to the holders and to any parish in which they took up residence. In March 1727, the Colerne overseers paid 5s 0d for a meeting when it was "agreed to warn . . . . . . intruders to bring certificates or depart".

There are no actual certificates to be found among the Colerne records, but some relating to people with Colerne settlements have been preserved by other parishes. One such certificate, dated 26th August 1699, states that "Stephen Showreing of our pish [parish] of Cullerne . . . . . is desirous to work and reside in your pish of Bradford . . . . . . for his better maintenance and livelyhood" and certifies that he is an "Inhabitant legally settled in our said pish of Cullerne". The importance and seriousness of this process can be deduced from the fact that it is not only signed and sealed by Mr Showring himself, two churchwardens and two overseers, but is also countersigned by two Justices of the Peace.

The need for settlement certificates was greatly reduced by the Act of 1795 which provided that people could not be removed until they became an actual charge on the parish. But the law of settlement and removal remained substantially in force until 1876, and there is evidence of its continued operation by the Chippenham Board of Guardians after they had come into existence in 1835.

Illegitimacy

Illegitimate children (always referred to as "bastards" in the records of this period) naturally tended to become a charge on the parish. Overseers sought to avoid this charge either by persuading the parents to marry (clearly not always possible) or by making the father pay for the upkeep of his child. It seems that, in general, the problem was

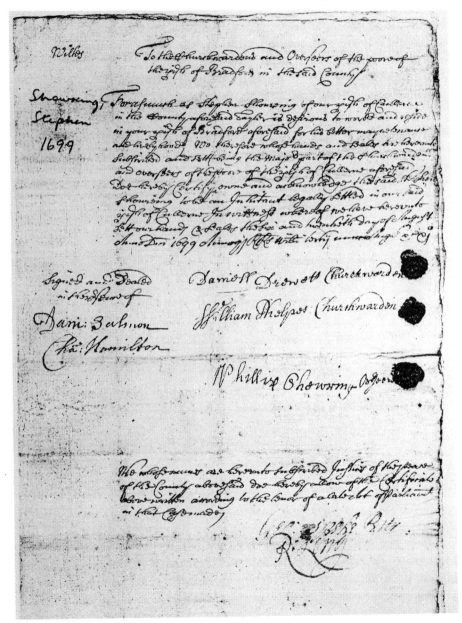

Fig 43   Settlement certificate for Stephen Showreing, 1699

dealt with in rural parishes without too much recourse to the rigours of the law (mothers of bastard children who became a charge *could* be sent to the house of correction); but the potential charge to the parish was considerable and the overseers naturally tried to avoid it.

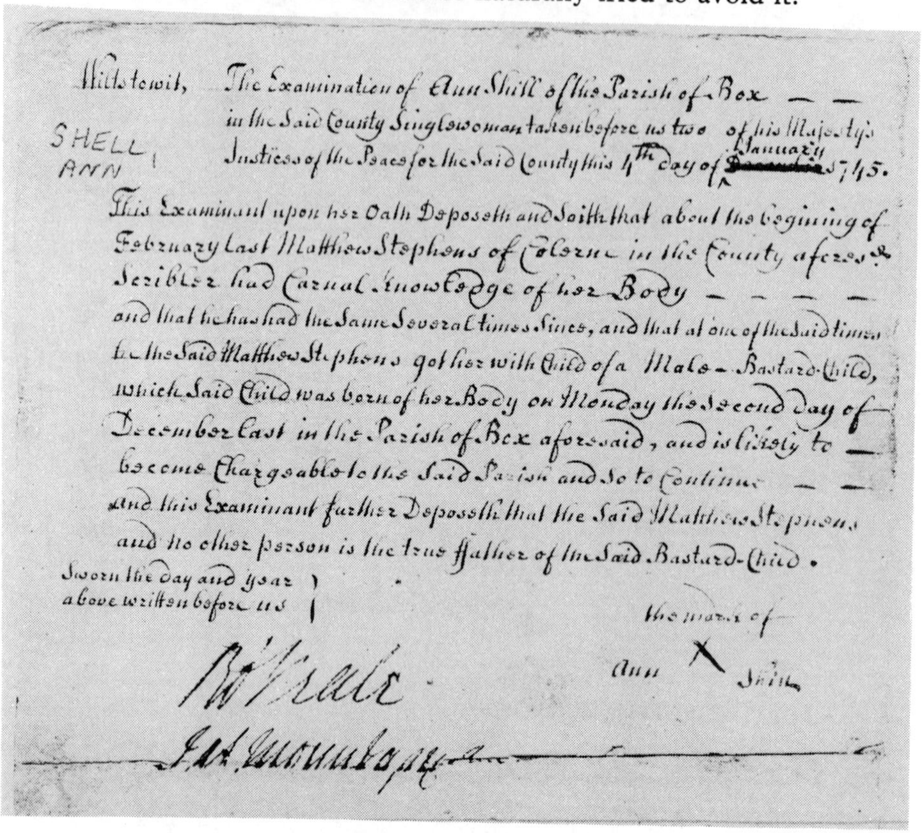

Wilts to wit, The Examination of Ann Shill of this Parish of Box in the Said County Singlewoman taken before us two of his Majesty's Justices of the Peace for the Said County this 4th day of January 1745.

SHELL ANN

This Examinant upon her Oath Deposeth and Saith that about the begining of February last Matthew Stephens of Colerne in the County aforesd Scribler had Carnal knowledge of her Body — and that he has had the Same Several times Since, and that at one of the Said times he the Said Matthew Stephens got her with Child of a Male Bastard-Child, which Said Child was born of her Body on Monday the second day of December last in the Parish of Box aforesaid, and is likely to become Chargeable to the Said Parish and So to Continue — And this Examinant further Deposeth that the Said Matthew Stephens and no other person is the true ffather of the Said Bastard-Child.

Sworn the day and year above written before us

the mark of Ann X Shill

Fig 44 Ann Shill's bastardy examination, 1745

There are references to bastardy, magistrates' examinations of the mother to determine paternity, and payments for upkeep by the fathers in both our sets of overseers' accounts. The Wiltshire archives also include the record of one such examination in 1745 of Ann Shill of the parish of Box who said that "about the beginning of February last Mathew Stephens of Colerne . . . . had Carnal knowledge of her Body

and he has had the same several times since" and that he got her
with child who was born on 2nd December and "is likely to become
chargeable to the said Parish and so to continue". The document was
sworn before two Justices who both signed it together with the mark
of Ann Shill. This is only a record of the mother's examination; a
bastardy certificate on a printed form of 1768 indicates that an order
would be made after the reputed father had also been examined. That
these proceedings could take some time is shown by the fact that this
certificate is dated more than eleven months after the birth of the
child. The delay was the result of the reputed father attempting to
evade his responsibility; a warrant for his apprehension which is also
preserved had been issued by a JP in Corsham a month before the
order was made.

A coherent account of some of these proceedings emerges from the
nineteenth century records. In August 1807 we have:

Hannah Holways Examination and warrant	4s 0d
Journey and expences to Do.	7s 0d
Apprehending of Benjamin Harris, the reputed	
Father of the Child Expences etc.	10s 6d
Constable keeping se[same?] in Custody	3s 6d

and among the overseers' receipts:

Received of Benjamin Harris a Compensation for a	
Bastard of Hannah Holway, according to the order	
and decree of a Vestry held this day	£15 0s 0d

A similar account of examinations and apprehension in 1818 ends
with the overseers paying for the marriage of the parties concerned:
9s 0d for the wedding ring etc and 3s 0d for the clerk's fees. It has
been suggested that overseers sometimes offered to pay for the wedding as an incentive to the father to 'make an honest woman' of the
mother!

Entries like these are quite common in the records; and throughout
the early nineteenth century the accounts include payments to so-and-
so's bastard and receipts of money from some of the fathers.

Pauper badges

It is implicit in what we have already written that we have found very few instances of the harsher penalties of the early Poor Laws. The worst of these, which was in operation in the middle of the sixteenth century, actually involved the branding of vagrants and, for a second offence, their enslavement. This was soon abolished, but a later law of 1697 introduced a lesser indignity. This provided that all paupers, their wives and children should wear a badge on their right shoulder consisting of a large P and the initial letter of the name of their parish in red or blue cloth. The ostensible reason for this was to identify those who were receiving parish assistance to prevent them begging elsewhere. Paupers refusing to wear badges could be refused help or sent to the house of correction.

There is a reference to this practice in the Colerne overseers' accounts for December 1706 when they paid 4d for "Marks for the poor"; but we have not found any others until 1741–2:

June	Paid for 6 marks for the poor	3s 0d
Nov	Paid for 3 poore marks	1s 6d
Feb	A Parish mark for Mary House	6d
	For 2 marks for Hana Tiler and Frederick Sherell	1s 0d

It appears probable that the wearing of badges had not been strictly enforced during the preceding 35 years. Unfortunately, 1742 is the year when this account book comes to an end, so we do not know how long it continued. The legislation was only repealed in 1810, but there is no mention of badges in the later Colerne accounts which begin in 1805.

The Colerne Poor House

By March 1836 John Horseman, whom we mentioned earlier, was certainly living in the "Colerne Workhouse". The minutes of the Chippenham Guardians of the Poor list him as one of several people who were to be removed from that institution because they were closing it down. One of their first acts, in December 1835, had been to review the existing provision of workhouses in their area. There were five, at Chippenham, Corsham, Lacock, Box and Colerne, and they soon decided that those in Corsham, Box and Colerne were surplus to their needs. Colerne was the smallest of these; according to the minutes of 18th December 1835, it then held eighteen persons and although it could accommodate 35, it had never had more than 24.

Surprisingly, there is no clear indication of the existence of this workhouse in the accounts of the Colerne overseers. A workhouse had been established in Bristol by an Act of 1695–6 and thereafter in various other towns; but they do not appear to have been set up in many rural areas prior to 1722–3 when there was a general Act permitting them to be established by any parish or group of parishes. Their purpose was to provide lodging and employment for the poor, and able-bodied people who refused to enter the workhouse were to lose their entitlement to relief.

The Colerne overseers' accounts for 1737 have this entry for 29th October: "Pd Robert Ralins for his house that was bought for the yous of the parish: £5 4s 0d", but a building described as the "Church House" existed even earlier, as the following entries show:

1712	Sept	Expenses when mett about the Church house	4s 3d
	Dec	For Glazing the Church house	8s 9d
		For wattling in the Church house	2s 6d

In 1713 there were expenses amounting to some £3 0s 0d in all for tiling the Church House and more repairs to the windows in 1714 and 1718. In March 1719 there were expenses "for and about woman that was in the Church House". These were all prior to the general Act to establish workhouses; but the last of these entries, in particular, certainly implies that the Church House was used for lodging poor people, if not actually as a 'workhouse'. In fact, poor houses where the impotent poor could live without the obligation to work had been mentioned as early as the Act of 1601, so it seems likely that this Church House was one such building and the house acquired in 1737 may have been another, rather than an actual workhouse.

The enclosures map of 1787 shows three houses in the village which are described as "poor house". One was in Watergates beside the churchyard, where some people still remember the village fire engine and bier being kept; the other two were on the west side of Totts Lane (now Silver Street) approximately where the bungalows now stand. These are probably the buildings which are described in the Guardians' minutes as the Colerne workhouse. Whether they ever had any stringent regulations about working is doubtful; certainly J Horseman does not appear to have been capable of work when he was housed there.

Even with this certain knowledge of the existence of the Colerne poor houses, it is difficult to establish any clear reference to them in the overseers' accounts for 1805–32. Towards the end of this period they were making annual payments of rent to a number of people. In 1828–9, where it is set out very clearly, there were nine such payments amounting to £45 0s 0d in all. Presumably these were all for housing the poor but whether any of the properties would have been called a poor house is not clear. Perhaps the best clues occur in 1806–7. In that year the accounts, kept by Collatinus Rawlings, record:

Paid Miss Ladd one years rent for C. Isaac	£3 10s 0d
Mr. Pinchin's House rent for Wicks, Gilman	
Tyley and Smith	£7 16s 0d
William Rawlins rent for Clarke	£1 11s 6d

and in the next year there are the same payments to Mrs Ladd and Mr Pinchin but (presumably for the same Clarke):

James Clark's house rent in Tots Lane	£3 3s 0d

We already know that Mrs Ladd was C Isaac's landlady at Kingsdown; but Mr Pinchin's house which accommodated four people (and their families?), and for which rent was paid right up to 1832, is a possible candidate for the name "poor house", and James Clark was certainly housed in Totts Lane.

Another strange element in this story is that the Guardians' minutes name Thomas Salter as the "present Governor" of the Colerne workhouse and in March 1836 they paid him £8 0s 0d for the performance of that office during the preceding quarter, yet there are no comparable payments in the overseers' accounts. The only plausible explanation we can offer is that he was appointed (perhaps in a tidying-up exercise prior to the Guardians taking over) between our last overseers' accounts in January 1832 and the minutes of December 1835.

Poor houses (i.e. houses used by the parish to accommodate people in receipt of poor relief) certainly existed in Colerne, probably by the early eighteenth century. Whether these ever became workhouses, in the sense in which the term was used after 1834, remains unclear.

Other duties of the overseers

Like other parishes, Colerne made use of the poor rate to collect funds for other parish duties besides the relief of the poor. Although these functions are not strictly within our subject matter, and were always a very small part of the overseers' expenditure, we shall give a brief account of some of them in this section.

We have already referred to expenditure on repairs to roads, bridges, the Fosse wall (presumably a road boundary), and at Duncombe (on the Fosse Way). The repair of highways, which had been a manorial function, became a parish duty under an Act of 1555 and parishioners were required to contribute transport and labour to carry it out. The work was supposed to be supervised by unpaid 'surveyors of highways', at first appointed by the parish, but after 1691 appointed by the justices from a list provided by the parish. This system did not come to an end until a new Act in 1835; but it was much neglected in many parts of the country in the seventeenth and eighteenth centuries. A highway rate was authorised in 1654 but was often included in the poor rate. This would account for the expenditures on roads by the overseers and they may have employed poor people to do some of the work.

Another of the old manorial responsibilities which devolved upon the overseers – but this time by custom rather than specific legislation – was the supervision of the open-field system of agriculture. Under this system, where fields were divided into strips with many different holders and each landholder had his strips scattered in different fields, someone had to have responsibility for coordinating the cultivation, destroying vermin etc. This accounts for entries such as those for "keeping the fields" and "powder and shot" in the period before the main Colerne enclosures.

One of the most ancient parish offices was that of Constable, dating back at least to the thirteenth century. Originally appointed by the manors, they were later appointed by the Vestries (and confirmed by the magistrates) in many places, and their functions often overlapped those of the overseers. In the accounts for 1716 we find:

Sept	to Mr. Organ Constable for Goall [gaol] and Mar-shalls and Vagrants	£1 6s 0d
Dec	to Charles Hamilton to carry Watts to prison	£1 12s 3d
	Paid to Daniel Blathleys wife for her Husbands Horses and time for watts being carried to prisson	£1 0s 0d

and in the following month Watts' wife was paid 10s 0d poor relief.

Other payments include one for repair of the village stocks (10s 0d) in 1720, another for "two pair of handbolts" [handcuffs?] (12s 0d) in 1828, and purchases of constable's staves in 1815 and 1820, as well as other instances of people being taken to prison.

Another of the constable's functions which became mixed with the overseers' was his responsibility for the Militia. Until 1757 the duty of providing military service had rested with individuals but it was then devolved to the parish. The names of men to serve in the militia, for three years each, were drawn by lot, but this service could be avoided by paying for a substitute. The Colerne overseers' accounts include payment of the militia bounty (e.g. £10 0s 0d each to M Sumsion and D Aust in June 1808), payments to the families of substitutes, and in 1807 entries relating to a man who absconded:

Dec	Journey to Chippenham attending the Justices relating to William Wicks he being drawn in the Militia	5s 0d
	Advertising of William Wicks in the three Bath public papers two weeks and having hand bills printed for apprehending	£3 1s 6d
	distributing Bills by divers Coachmen	10s 0d

Another of the odd jobs usually performed by the constable was the care of the parish bull, a very important creature for the villagers who owned cows. The accounts for 1819–20 record "Several Journeys to Box after Bullock: 2s 0d" and there are similar entries in other years, so presumably Colerne did not have its own parish bull at this time.

Later, there were newly created responsibilities which also fell on the overseers, at least temporarily. The first national Census was taken in 1801 and it has been taken every ten years since, except in 1941. There are no overseers' accounts for 1801 but there are entries in both 1811 and 1821 for expenses in "makeing out the Population".

Another nineteenth century innovation was vaccination against smallpox. In 1829–30 there must have been a special campaign in Colerne; the doctor was paid £5 5s 0d for vaccination in addition to his usual fee of £10 10s 0d (and a little later the Chippenham Guardians were also making regular payments for vaccinations).

Conclusion

As we have examined these old books of the overseers, we have been struck by how many aspects of our modern provision for the poorest members of society have their parallels in those earlier days. The biggest differences lie in the purely punitive elements of the Elizabethan poor law and its very local administration by the parish, in contrast with today's mainly national provision. It was this parish responsibility for its own poor – and the resulting necessity to avoid paying for paupers who were 'settled' elsewhere – which led to the apparent harshness of some of the removals which took place. Such a case occurred in May 1717 when an entry reads:

> Then did the majority of the pish Agree to Stand by the Churchwardens and Overseers Concerning an order to be taken to Carry of Ann the reputed wife of John Watts Lately deceased.

It appears that, being only the "reputed" wife, she had not established settlement in Colerne, but nevertheless this decision was sufficiently controversial to require confirmation by a Vestry meeting. On the other side of the coin we have already seen that the overseers were quite often prepared to enter into agreements with other parishes to pay for relief for paupers with Colerne settlements, and so avoid the upheaval of their removal.

All in all, our impression of the administration of the poor laws in Colerne prior to 1834 is that potentially harsh laws were interpreted relatively humanely. Some of this evidence is admittedly negative – the absence of references to the harsher penalties – but there is also much that is positive in the instances we have given of the treatment of the sick, the elderly, the unemployed and the poorly paid. We certainly would not claim that Colerne was alone in this, but we feel that it was indeed a caring community.

How things changed for the village poor after 1834, when they were no longer cared for by their own parish but became the responsibility of the Chippenham Board of Guardians (covering more than thirty parishes), is a subject for further study.

Sources

Tate W E, *The Parish Chest* (3rd edn.), Phillimore & Co. Ltd. Chichester, 1983.

Colerne Poor Books, 1688–1742, 1805–18 and 1819–32. Wiltshire Record Office

Colerne Churchwarden's Account Book, 1755–1868. Wiltshire Record Office.

Chippenham Board of Guardians Minute Books, 1835–38. Wiltshire Record Office.

Colerne School in this Century

Audrey Woods

The School in 1900

The first day of January 1900 saw the opening of the new school term. Teacher in charge at the infant department was Mrs Jane Phillips, whilst the head teacher of the day and continuation schools was Mr J A B Taylor.

The infant department held 97 children, aged from three to seven years with two teachers and a pupil teacher, and 160 children from seven to fourteen years attended the day school with two teachers and, usually, three pupil teachers. A continuation school was held each evening of the week by Mr Taylor, and Clara Aldridge took the sewing group in this evening school. There were only twelve students, who had to be either over fourteen years or to have passed the fifth standard.

At the middle of the year Mr Taylor left and was replaced by George Amos and his wife, aged 44 and 38 respectively. Indications are that there was a much tighter control of paperwork, building and pupils following the change.

The infant department occupied the whole south end of the school. There were 90 pupils. Forty sat in the main room (perhaps that is the northern classroom) and 30 occupied the small room.

Lessons for the infants consisted of Writing, Arithmetic, Reading and Needlework. What the results were and how lessons were taught is left to the imagination, although twice a year a note in the logbook mentions that a "new book for each division" has been distributed, so we can be pretty sure everybody in the class read the same book, probably aloud and in turn around the rows.

Fig 45   The old school and a group photograph, c1900

Infants also had an 'object' lesson once a week when the pupil teacher prepared a subject to give to all the children together. We know what the children learnt about – sheep, cat, horse, squirrel, snail, swallow, skylark, cuckoo, blackbird, ostrich, cork, sponge, daisy, buttercup, hedgehog, bat and mole.

It can be presumed that the basic course was followed in the day school with older pupils. There was also emphasis, by George Amos, on repetition lessons. This was recitation and learning by heart. The different standards (one to six) learnt different poems such as "The Gladiator", "Stately homes of England" and "Who made me?"

Shortly after George Amos commenced at the school he began attracting more boys – and young men – to the continuation school by conducting simple science experiments. This appears to have fired enthusiasm and eventually 25 'lads' were in regular attendance. Subjects were Drawing (plans and elevations), Singing, Woodcarving, Woodwork, Commercial Arithmetic, Commercial Geography; sessions were from about 7pm to 9pm and two subjects were taught for one hour each on each evening the school was open.

Attendance at the infant and day school was poor. Any rain or snow made conditions on the paths into the village poor and, very often, only village children came to school. Both the head of the infant department and the main school made constant complaints to the school board and found that the board did nothing at all about the situation. The weather in early 1900 was so bad that the infants had no playtime session outside from November 1899 until March of 1900 (although it must be said that the 'playground' appears to have been the road outside the school building at that time).

Apart from absences for bad weather the children were kept at home when diphtheria struck, or other diseases such as whooping cough, chicken pox and a smallpox scare (perhaps a measles outbreak as there is no record of any child actually contracting the disease).

The school was frequently closed for official half days as well as the statutory school holidays. Each last Friday of the month meant a holiday in the afternoon. All church festivals, Whitsun, Ascension, Patronal and St Matthias meant an afternoon holiday, as did the last day of the school year when there was the annual treat and prize giving at Lucknam Park. Harvest Festival called for a half day and a local wedding saw the school closed also. Half holidays came after a period of good attendance, peace in South Africa – in 1902 – and a whole day's holiday came every November when the Clothing Club was held in the school. Holidays were also given for haymaking and potato picking. By 1902 George Amos settled down to bring better order to the school. He visited his Union representative in Chippenham to seek advice about rowdiness in and around the school and promptly informed the 25 'lads' at the continuation school that the school "will be terminated" unless behaviour improved.

The continuation school now had a new timetable which gave no lessons on Friday evenings but two a night on the other four evenings. For girls there was Needlework and Cookery (which followed the Wiltshire Syllabus). The boys had History (the growth and expansion of the British Empire from 1475); Drawing (freehand, modelling, geometry and brushwork); Geography (Babylon, Phoenician, Ionian, Rome, Venice, Portugal, Holland and England); Nature (wild flowers, birds, insects, animals, minerals, rock formation and oolite); Woodwork, and finally, Social Intercourse. Within a year the pupils following this last course were down to ten.

Day school lessons continued with senior girls being sent into the infant department to help when teachers were absent. Some were sent home because their hair was messy. Some strong words were used by both parents and headteacher, but the girls seem to have complied with demands and returned within a week.

In 1902 the playground between the building and churchyard was asphalted and infants, girls and boys could take it in turns to go out into the fresh air at morning and afternoon playtimes. But battles went on about the coal fired stoves which consistently failed to heat rooms to an adequate temperature in the winter months. George Amos frequently reported temperatures of 45°F when he felt they should be 56–60°F.

The year 1902 was the beginning of a few years of successes at the Chippenham Show with prizes for needlework, dress and pinafore making, and the boys had first and second prizes in brushwork.

In 1903 pressure was again put upon the school board to combat the unnecessary absences of pupils. Three parents were taken before Corsham Magistrates and fined for the non-attendance of their children. It had some effect but George Amos continued to send out notes to parents warning them what might happen if attendance was not regular.

In 1904 there were battles between headteacher, managers and school cleaner over cleaning toilets, access to coal supplies and keeping the temperature at a reasonable level in classrooms. At the Colerne Flower Show seventeen out of eighteen prizes for drawing were taken by boys, and nine out of ten needlework prizes were taken by girls from the school. Mr Amos, a keen gardener, took four first prizes and three seconds at the horticultural stand. No wonder he requested a plot of land for the school boys to learn gardening and was bitterly upset when Wiltshire County Council turned down his request. He also felt annoyed at a new Arithmetic scheme introduced by the County as it was hard to implement with his inadequate staffing arrangements. He had disagreements with staff and one member transferred to the Infant school. Resignations were offered by Mr and Mrs Amos, but by the end of 1905 all was calm again.

The official punishment book began in 1906 – usually one or two 'stripes' for misbehaviour and disobedience for boys, girls or infants. Maybe once a week someone was in trouble, but things got out of control by 1906 when there was impudent behaviour, lawlessness, mischief and mud throwing at windows in the village (mostly, it seems, by girls). "Home influence is definitely bad" said George Amos.

The continuation school had slowly been losing pupils. A lantern exhibition and concert are mentioned as "drawing the lads away" and a local club proved a strong counter-attraction. Many boys found employment out of the village and, after a sad message "I have done my best", the last entry referring to the continuation school comes on 16th January 1907.

Day school children were mentioned as being badly behaved, truanting, throwing ink, whistling, playing in toilets. The headteacher had trouble with his eyes and attended hospital and finally Mr and Mrs Amos left the school on 8th April 1909 – just as medical examinations were beginning for all school children.

Mr Tucker's reign

Ada Pallin took charge until June, when Archie Tucker began his duties as headteacher. In April 1910 the infants were amalgamated into Colerne Mixed and Infant School.

Mr Tucker settled in to face the annual Religious Instruction examination – always a favourable report – and the medical examination day in October with an upheaval of the running of the school. Most children had to' be weighed and measured before the day the medical officer was due to attend.

The battle of the cleaner versus headteacher continued. There were complaints of broken windows left unrepaired, dusty desks, fires not lit and ink jars smashed during cleaning.

Formal arrangements were made for the use of playground:

1. The playground will be open at 8.45 a.m. and 1 p.m. to all children except those in the infant division.
2. Boys to go in the playground on arrival except on wet days when they shelter in their lobby till the arrival of the teachers.
3. Girls to go in the playground when the turret bell rings (8.55 and 1.25) except on wet days.
4. Infants may enter their classroom on the arrival of one of their teachers.
5. Each teacher in turn for a week at a time to be responsible for the discipline during recreation time.
6. Boys and infants (at different times) use the playground for recreation: girls may play in the road between the girls entrance and the playground door, must proceed to the playground when the turret bell rings.

September 1911 saw the opening of school, with a recurrence of non-attendance and a flurry of reminder notes. Parents excused themselves either because of a smell of paint in the school or because they didn't know school had begun again!

At some time between 1911 and 1912 gas lighting must have been installed and great care was taken to record how many burners were used between 3 and 4 pm each day.

There was trouble with the cleaner again in 1913. She forgot to dust maps and pictures, did not report a broken pane of glass and did not remove graffiti that appeared in the toilets during the Christmas holiday. But the teachers too were in trouble and were reported to the managers, after the end of term exams in December, as "weak and unsufficient". It was also proving difficult to attract new members of staff "owing to isolation of village and its distance from the railway".

The First World War

Mr Tucker faced some difficulties in 1914. He was needed frequently by neighbours to help with swarms of bees. He coped with these by leaving school with some of his more senior pupils and rehousing the bees in his own skeps.

There was an unfavourable report from inspectors, referring to the buildings and standards of behaviour and work.

By 1915 troubles included smelly and dirty pupils, head lice, sick staff and continual absences of various pupils, scarlet fever and whooping cough.

In November 1915 the headteacher began his long battle for acceptance in the army. But his school was steadily increasing in numbers, especially the younger 'babies' of three to five years and everyone was hopeful that the school would keep its staff of six.

In 1917 there were bee swarms, chestnut picking at Lucknam (one ton picked), blackberry gathering (119 lbs collected), and the first mention of a school dentist who looked at the teeth of all between six and eight years of age.

In October 1918 there were six half-day holidays for blackberry picking and then a half holiday for Armistice Day, with half the school continuing the absence the next day also.

Between the wars

Work continued with many changes of staff. Women teachers left for new posts or marriage and a fair number of uncertificated teachers were found to be unsuitable and left after one or two terms' work.

Calamity hit the village in January 1924. The first case of diphtheria was notified at school on 24th January and three days later the school was closed. The epidemic lasted until 17th March with seventeen children still excluded, and in that time eighteen children had contracted diphtheria and four had died. The school was sprayed and fumigated before re-opening.

There was a surprising amount of movement of children in and out of the village. In 1925 the new entrants included one child from a private school, six whose parents had moved in from other towns and villages and eighteen new pupils from the village population. Three-

year-olds were still being admitted and children left at fourteen years
unless they reached standard five before this time. They left to
commence work and some passed exams for promotion to various
higher schools, including Dauntsey Agricultural, King Edward's,
Bath Art School, Bath Technical School, Chippenham School and
Trowbridge Secretarial School.

In 1927 an inspector's report was generally favourable, but the
standard of drawing was obviously lower than in the heyday of George
Amos and reading standards in the infant department were not felt to
be very high.

Half holidays seem to have disappeared by 1928 and only adverse
weather conditions meant 'no school'! But school trips were now
thought about. There was a visit to Wembley for two days for the
Empire Exhibition in 1924, a cinema trip in 1928, and in 1929 a
flagstaff was erected in the playground and the Union flag raised for
Empire Day, Armistice Day and other special occasions.

More and more health care was given. There were regular medical
inspections, dental treatment and, in 1929, remedial exercises were a
regular weekly occurrence.

In 1931 a water supply for the village was discussed and the school
was closed in the morning for a public meeting to take place. Despite
various outings, closures and the difficulty of obtaining staff, by 1932 a
most favourable report is given in the inspection of that year. "Friend-
liness, steadiness and attention" – so Mr Tucker's tough lines were
paying off!

The Second World War

Mr Tucker's period as headteacher ended in 1939. His last entry is for
31st October. He returned in January 1940 for the presentation of a
gramophone and picnic basket. Fred Bedford commenced on 8th
January 1940 and started to complain about the cleaner on that first
day. And by the end of the month he had started what appears to be
the first games periods on the recreation ground. Previous to this any
physical exercise was in the form of 'drill' in the playground. There
were many canings for bystanders pulling faces and generally making
fun of participants.

Alarums and excursions were caused through most of 1940 over the sirens and what children and staff must do. Stay in school, go to church, run home – ARP wardens said one thing and County Education committee another. Then four sirens could be heard. Which one to obey – Box, Bath, Chippenham, RAF?

On 18th June there was the arrival of nine pupils evacuated from Walthamstow. September saw regular arrangements instituted, but children were scattered in cloakrooms, classrooms, rectory shelter and sent home if within three minutes running distance. On 13th September, children took cover in school as two bombs fell 'in the vicinity'. The RAF siren sounded immediately(!) afterwards and the 'raiders past' signal was some fifteen minutes later. On 17th September, a damaged Spitfire landed at the RAF station, but there were no bombs and no one was hurt. On the 25th, a large number of aircraft flew overhead and everyone took cover. Two bombs were dropped at 9.50 pm outside the village on 19th November, but there were no casualties or damage. In October, at last, the start of a garden to help "Dig for Victory" – how pleased George Amos would have been.

The year 1941 got off to a sad start with a plane crashing, and killing the pilot, at Watergates Villa. The explosion caused all to take cover and, after school, the older children assisted the fire brigade to extinguish the fire. In March and April sandbags were placed at all entrances to school and gas masks worn and tested.

Throughout the war years visiting speakers came to talk about camouflage, identification of planes, dangers of high explosives, and many men from the RAF came to help with sports and plays, and taught the classes in the absence of staff members. Milk was available from 1942 – free if family circumstances showed it was needed.

On 27th April 1942 many children were absent. This followed the weekend air raid on Bath and most had spent two sleepless nights. Three families were still concerned and refused to send their children to school at all. In July news came of the headteacher's son being killed in the Middle East and added distress came five days later when an infant died after a tonsillectomy.

First swimming lessons – for girls only – at Widdenham in the brook began in July 1943. School children were needed for work on farms. Schools opened late in September to leave pupils free to aid in harvest and older children were released from class work to farmers "who applied in writing".

In June 1943 talks began on the serving of school dinners, but a date to start was not given although the staff were opposed to the idea and found many difficulties.

Mr Bedford became ill in November 1942 and finally resigned on 17th February 1944 with a heart condition. He died on 15th June of that year. Mrs Richardson was acting headteacher until the arrival of the new headteacher, Andrew Walbank, on 17th April 1944. Mrs Walbank spent much time in the school as a supply class teacher when staff were absent.

Post-war expansion

Things changed quite rapidly, with more excursions for the older children and frequent trips to Corsham for films, art shows, plays and concerts. Money was raised, and exceeded set targets, for 'Wings for Victory', 'Salute the Soldier' and 'National Savings'. A second allotment was taken over by the school with tools, plants, fruit trees and seeds supplied, in part, by the County. The County also supplied bicycles – on long loan – to children living at Thickwood. Waste of administrative time was resented, as children were weighed and measured because children over average size for their age were allocated extra clothing coupons. Two days holiday were allocated for V.E. Day, 8th May 1945. Road safety was considered and the police gave a talk on this in April 1946. In the reorganisation of Education, the school was designated Voluntary Controlled. The icy and prolonged winter of 1947 meant no fuel, no heating and only seniors came to school. In February 1947 the first child entered from the RAF married quarters. From then on came reports of numbers of schools attended by pupils, attempts to organise buses from Thickwood and a lack of cooperation with the RAF, as the head was never kept informed when 50 or 60 pupils would not arrive owing to camp parties, leaves or outings.

The first intimation of a school meals service having met with instant and complete opposition, plans went ahead for a canteen in 1948. In 1951 another room was looked for.

In 1952 the playground was tarmacadamed – in term time, to Mr

Walbank's rage – and tar was brought into the school. By 1st May the number on roll had grown to 182; all classes had to move forward seven pupils to take in the bulge, and a year later down it dropped to 169. The last fifteen-year-old attended school and left in 1953. Mrs Walbank fell over a milk crate, and her accident brought about an absence of 50 weeks. Tragically, by November 1955 she had become ill again and died. On 27th July 1956, Mr Walbank left Colerne School – to be succeeded on 31st August by Eric Chown with five other members of staff; there were about 180 on roll.

Fig 46   School group, 1961

The new school

Plans for the new Primary School arrived in January 1957. Part of the rectory garden was used as a school garden. In July there came the first of the annual outings to Bristol Zoo by the infant department, and then the first recorded break-in on the school premises. Over £6 went missing.

In 1958 no new children could be admitted due to lack of space. Eventually a room in the Rectory was taken over to hold a class of twenty. Eight staff members were employed from September 1958 and in October the new school opened with two infant classes. But numbers increased so rapidly that four years later the staff increased to ten with a non-teaching head and a roll of 270. A Pratten hut was opened on the 'new' school site in November but classes at the older end of school were still very overcrowded.

The commencement of 1963 saw snow, blizzards and such heavy frosts that frozen pipes stopped toilets flushing, and the school was virtually closed for normal education until about 6th February. In April the roll was 329, and three huts had to be used on the RAF site by October. All the while, building was continuing on the new site.

In January 1964 the third classroom (the single storey block) opened on the new site. By the end of 1964 the new school was ready and in January 1965 children were moved from temporary classrooms into the new school. Two rooms remained in use on the old school site. In May so many new infant entrants came that a third class had to be used on the original site. The dedication and official opening of the new school building took place on Friday, 21st May 1965 and was followed by a day's holiday to celebrate the event!

In September 1965 a form of 'Continuation' started with adult Floral Decoration and Keep Fit classes. Even more pupils arrived in April 1966 and another class was made in the dining room.

Mr Chown had been sick for some three years and continued work with help from his wife and friends. He died, very suddenly, on 28th February 1967. The acting headteacher, Audrey Woods, recently appointed as deputy head, was sanctioned by County Hall. Another single 'portable' classroom was erected on the main school site to cope with increased numbers.

In 1968, Edwin Haycroft became headteacher, and on 11th September of that year the P.T.A. was formed. There were many more 'out of school' activities, with educational trips to museums, concerts, a butter factory, London, Rode bird park and such like. School life went on with various changes – more music, italic handwriting, more visits to link with lessons. In September 1976 the RAF left and caused a drop of 100 in the school roll. Two teachers were redeployed and the

Fig 47   Last day at the old school, July 1976

Fig 48   'Grand Slam' cycling proficiency test, c1978/79

old school building was vacated on 23rd July. In 1977 a photo copier machine was delivered: just 70 years previously George Amos had been refused an "ink-copying machine" for his continuation classes to help him prepare work for 'the lads'. Numbers fluctated and a double mobile room was brought in during January 1978.

During a second break-in, two cameras, binoculars and tins of money were taken from filing cabinets. This was a sad end to the headship of Edwin Haycroft who left on 20th July 1979.

Rene Suter commenced as head on 4th September 1979 but one year later she entered hospital for major surgery and Audrey Woods once again acted as headteacher for just one term. At this time parents began to be encouraged to come into school, talk to staff and help with organising books and work on craft projects. This continued with the return of Mrs Suter. A school bookshop was started in 1981 and cycling proficiency lessons were held after school. At the beginning of 1982, the school was once again closed due to freezing conditions, snow, blocked roads and then frozen pipes. Children could come to collect work from staff who came in but conditions were too cold and unhygienic to remain. In November 1982 a 'Plant a Tree' event saw every child in the school planting a tree seed or sapling and in June 1984 the first strike by teachers meant the school closed for three days.

In 1985 a scheme of introducing children to their secondary school began – the fourth year pupils went to Corsham Comprehensive School for three days to attend classes and get a feel of the larger school. At the same time rising five-year-olds also began coming into school in the infant department for half a day for a few weeks.

Sources

Logbooks: Continuation School 1894–1904
    Infant School 1894–1910
    School 1910–1936 and 1936–1987
Wiltshire County Archive, Trowbridge.

"A Remarkably Healthy State"

Barrie and Janet Austin

It is a cause for amazement that we now quite take for granted that fresh, 'clean' water will flow from our taps, and our toilets will flush away all the 'nasties'. Yet it was only in 1848 that the Board of Health was set up for improving water supplies and drainage, and keeping towns clean. Edwin Chadwick, a barrister and member of the Board, fought for years to get a decent water supply and sanitation brought to London. Other cities and towns gradually followed his example. This was a slow business and it was not surprising that illnesses and epidemics, including the dreaded cholera, were frequent. Villages were very low on the list for improvement. Colerne's turn did not come until the 1930s, and then only for water. In July 1931 the Water Supplies and Sanitary Committee of the Chippenham Rural District Council sorrowfully concluded, "having regard to the heavy burden which the cost of the proposed water scheme will entail, the same being beyond the ability of the Parish to bear without assistance from the County Council and District Council... the Committee considered it impracticable to proceed at present with a scheme of Sewage and Sewage Disposal for the Parish".

This was by no means the first attempt to get Colerne a sewage system: as early as 18th January 1876 the 'Inspector of Nuisances' was directed to "submit his proposals relating to a Proposed Drainage Scheme for part of the village". This was, no doubt, due in part to many complaints by parishioners, and in particular a letter written in 1875 by a Mr C W Ingle to the Local Government Board complaining of the "unsanitary condition of the village", blaming all on the neglect of the Inspector of Nuisances, one Mr A H Lapham. The Local Government Board had smartly passed the letter to the Rural Sanitary

Authority. Their Clerk was rather testily instructed to reply "that the bad condition of the drainage at Colerne had been frequently brought under the notice of the Board by the Inspector, that no blame whatsoever was to be attached to that officer in respect of the manner in which he had discharged his duties, that a great deal had been done to remedy the bad state of the drainage and that further steps were being taken in the matter so that the Board hoped to shortly carry out a systematic plan of Drainage throughout the village".

However, surprise, surprise, by October 1877, he, with the backing of the 'Relieving Officer', is reporting that they "are of the opinion that the Drainage of the village of Colerne is in such an improved condition that nothing further need be done, especially as the Village is in a remarkably healthy state at present, and that this is confirmed by the report of the Medical Officer of Health which has not had a single entry of complaint for many months past". A rosy picture which does not seem to have lasted; there were more complaints of both the drainage and water supply being bad in 1891 and 1895.

Finding water

With a general move towards improving supplies in the latter half of the nineteenth century, water diviners and well diggers were in great demand, and in Colerne the most celebrated of these were members of the Mullins family. John Mullins, born on 12th November 1838, was the second son of a stonemason who followed his father into the trade. It was whilst working on Sir John Orred's estate at Ashwick in Gloucestershire that he discovered he possessed a gift for water divining. This he soon exploited by way of a thriving sideline throughout Wiltshire, where he was renowned for sinking deeper wells and finding water where others before him had failed. As his fame spread wider he was able to give up his work as a mason, engaging himself instead in travel all over the country in search of more and more water.

Two of John's four sons inherited his talent, particularly Henry, who joined the firm on his 21st birthday. In 1894 the family described their experiences in a book, "The Divining Rod", published shortly before John's death. The business continued well into the twentieth century – there is record of Mr W J Mullins finding water at Beaumaris,

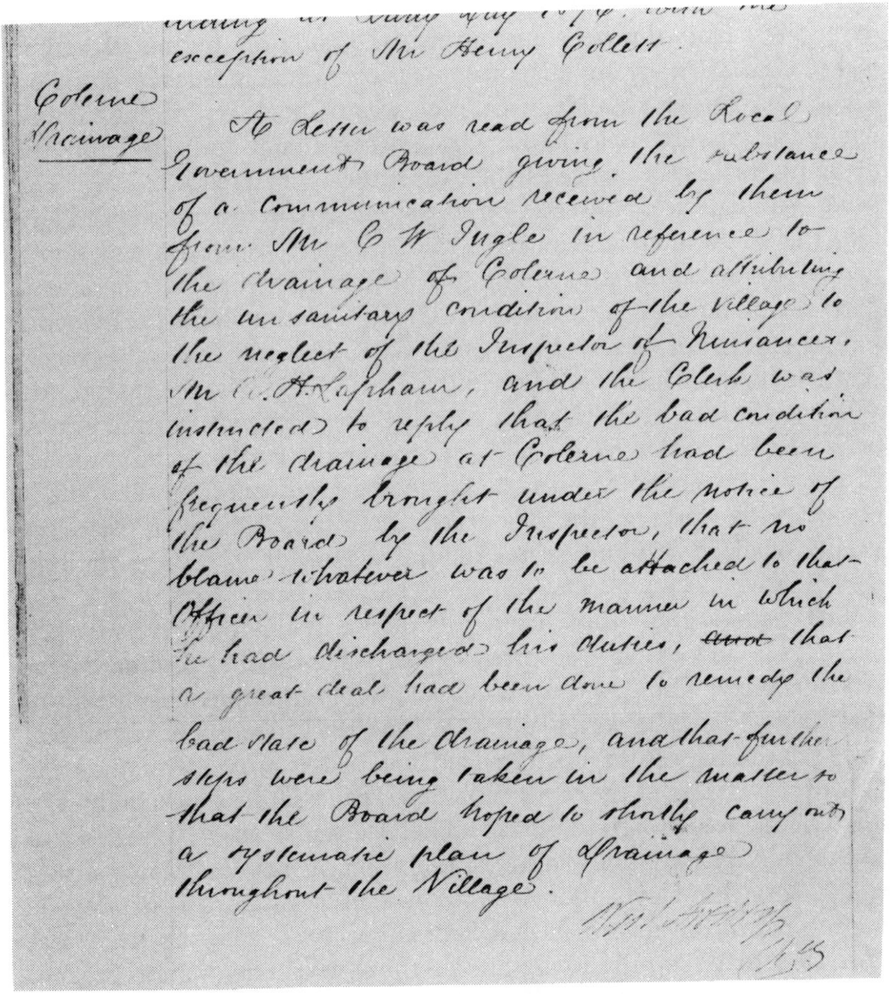

Fig 49   Extract from Minutes of Rural Sanitary Authority, 1875

Anglesey, for the BBC; not the sort of customer to spring immediately to mind in the more usual quest for pure, sweet water.

Water from the well

Whilst provision of more wells made life a little easier, on the whole things continued in much the same old way. Water was collected with great effort from the wells and springs and, later on, pumps. Where it was to be carried for any distance it was contained in buckets slung on a yoke across the shoulders. Storage was in buckets, 'dolly' tubs or whatever container was handy; an especially cool and clean one for drinking water was a large earthenware crock with a glazed lining. The used washing water trickled from the stone sink in the outside scullery into the stone-lined soakaway in the garden. The garden was also a handy repository for the 'night soil' where there was no convenient deep pit or hole in the rock upon which Colerne stands; allotments took their fair share too. Mr Horace Guy, who still lives in Colerne, remembers from his schooldays in the First World War the sexton, Mr William Holder, every evening carrying the buckets from the school privies, with a sack over them, down to a nearby garden to be emptied. A trustworthy schoolboy was despatched each morning to fill another bucket with water at the Watergates fountain: this dealt with the supply of clean drinking water for the school, or to sponge the odd grazed knee.

The mains water supply came to Colerne in 1935, but it had taken much time and effort – so often earlier attempts had foundered for lack of money. The Inspector was asked to report on the best means of improving Colerne's water supply in June 1891. August the same year saw the said Inspector reporting back that, in his opinion, an estimate of £31 for carrying out the work considered necessary was too high. The matter was accordingly deferred. These (August 1891) minutes also incidentally refer to complaints of pollution of the Watergates spring and of Mr Walmsley's offer to assist in their resolution. It is interesting to read in the record of 2nd September 1957, 66 years later, that "Mr Cheetham enquired whether anything would be done to prevent contamination of a water supply at Watergates, Colerne"!

It was not that the village was without its steady supply of water. In the 1890s the population of Colerne was estimated at roughly 975, 195 houses with five persons to a house. The Authorities were confident that three springs – Main Spring, Small Spring at Buttocks and Lictum Spring – could be depended upon to supply sufficient water, since they produced together about 31,000 gallons a day. What was needed was the help of two hydraulic rams which had to be capable of pumping 5000 gallons each a day to more accessible spots. On 20th

Fig 50   Ornamental surround of spring on Colerne Down

June 1892, the Inspector was set the task of finding out the cost of supplying and fixing all this magnificent machinery. In July 1893, a Local Government Board Inspector was unwise enough to proffer his advice as to the advisability of using an oil engine instead of rams. Mr Taylor, the owner of the property on which the rams would be built, did not view this at all favourably, feeling that it would pump the springs dry to the detriment of his farm, and he invited the Local Authority to purchase the land involved. In January 1894 it was decided in favour of rams. Why this ambitious plan was never carried

Fig 51   Village pond and well at Watergates

Fig 52   Watergates, 1990

out is a mystery which the minutes of the Water and Sanitation Committee do not reveal – perhaps it was dropped when the committee was wholly under the jurisdiction of Chippenham. A ram was built privately for Lucknam, and another by Mr John Walmsley to supply the Manor House at Colerne.

So the inhabitants of Colerne continued to plod to their wells, of which a 1905 map shows 41. The village pump, stone troughs and taps supplied from the springs were the alternatives. Mr Walmsley did have a tap put in his garden wall beside the Market Place so that the surplus from his private supply would be of benefit to the village, but this was a mere trickle compared to what was really needed. Standpipes followed, with water supplied from a pump at Widdenham driven from a waterwheel in the By Brook (the remains of which survive) but it was evident by the late 1920s that matters could not continue in this manner and plans were drawn up by the Chippenham RDC for a reservoir and mains water supply for Colerne. However, that was merely the start of the matter – in such schemes there are all the legal niceties: 'easements', 'rights of way', 'deeds of indemnity'. There was money to be raised to pay for it all from local and national government, including an improbably named 'Unemployment Grants Committee'. By July 1931, the Minister of Health stated that "the scheme was such as might be approved". This was no doubt influenced by the view expressed further on in his letter that "the necessity for the scheme had arisen through the practice of disposing of foul waste liquid by means of leaky cesspools, old wells and fissures in the rock, in consequence of which the underground water had been polluted".

There was much manoeuvring between RDC and landowners with private water supplies. Captain Grant, now owner of the Manor House, and his tenant, Captain Despard, agreed amicably to waive the right to receive and take water from their existing private supply and have their hydraulic ram maintained, in return for the Council providing a supply of water to the existing tanks and points in the Manor House. Mr Hoddinott of Euridge Manor Farm managed things equally nicely. Three water troughs to be provided, maintained and constantly supplied with water. There was even to be compensation for any disturbance whilst laying the service or if the water supply

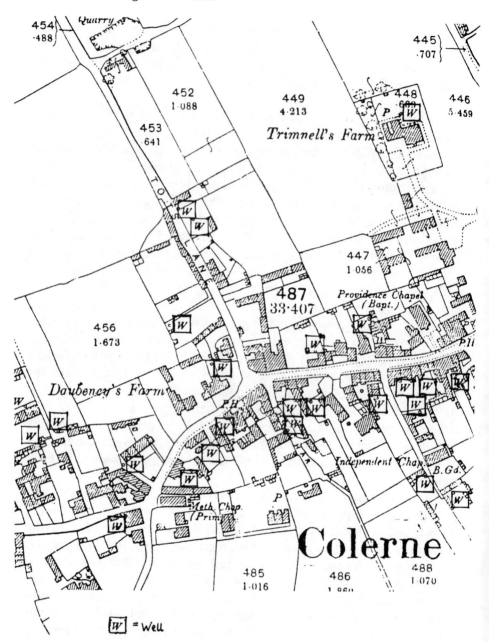

$\boxed{W}$ = Well

Fig 53   Some of the Colerne wells, 1905

failed. The Council were more wary over the supply of water to the farmhouse, three cottages and buildings: Mr Hoddinott was to foot the bill, but the pill was sweetened by their agreeing "to pay all proper costs and expenses of Mr Hoddinott".

Fig 54   Plaque in Manor House wall

Mr Grainger, agent for Lucknam Park Estate, did not fare so well. He enquired whether the new supply could be available for cottages on the estate and one at Thickwood hamlet without further cost, and the Lucknam Mansion if required. Mr R J Payne of Sydney Farm, Colerne, wished the water to be laid on to his farmhouse and buildings. The Committee replied promptly to Mr Grainger that whilst there was no engineering difficulty in complying with his wishes, the cost would be £1050, which they considered prohibitive. Likewise Mr Payne was informed that his premises could be supplied at a cost of £325. Mr Grainger expressed the opinion that the original scheme should have made provision for a supply to the hamlet of Thickwood. It was recorded in the minutes that "No action was taken".

Fig 55   Pump and trough in Tutton Hill

Work begins at last

Slowly, slowly the scheme moved forward. Messrs Parker, Pearson and Ross Hooper, Chartered Civil Engineers of Chippenham had submitted several feasibility reports, and by 25th May 1934 their plan for obtaining a water supply for Colerne from the Widdenham source was adopted by the Council. By November of the same year they had Ministerial approval, subject, as always, to the continuing bacteriological examination of the water from the Widdenham and surrounding springs proving it remained pure and uncontaminated. On 25th

May 1934, "The whole matter having been discussed in detail it was moved by Mr J Brooke seconded by Mr H T Maynard and resolved to recommend... that the method of charge to be made against the Parish of Colerne be to regard the Widdenham account as a joint one for the Parishes of Box, Corsham and Colerne, the expenditure to be chargeable proportionately against these parishes on the basis of the actual respective consumption of water".

The Engineers arranged for tenders to be invited. They regretted that a decision by the Council that the contractor should be required to employ 90 per cent local labour would not be practicable, and that an alternative should be that the contractor employ, *as far as possible*, men resident in the district. It was agreed that this would be more workable.

On 1st February 1935, the Clerk to the Council reported joyfully that a revised estimate by the Engineers for £7300 was £200 less than the original application made for a loan sanction. A tender from Mr E Ireland had been accepted provisionally and the Minister informed. The Minister was happy and the Engineers gave Mr Ireland formal notice to commence the work on 25th February. Mr C Saunders of Llanelly was appointed as Clerk of Works at an inclusive salary of £5 0s 0d per week, subject to two weeks' notice, his duties to commence on 28th February 1935.

The Ministry of Health was still agitated about the steps being taken to ensure protection of the water supply from all possible sources of human contamination. The Chippenham Medical Officer of Health recommended that samples of the water be submitted for bacteriological examination once a quarter for a period of one year.

The first Engineers' report of 29th March showed that 500 yards of trench had been opened and pipe laid. The total number of men engaged for this work was seventeen, amongst whom were eight Colerne men. The work progressed steadily but there was the odd, unforeseen, delay. A severe storm on 25th June loosened the ground where excavation had been made for the Widdenham reservoir, and it had to be built on firmer adjoining land.

The work did not meet with universal acclaim: Mr C Spirrell of Widdenham wanted to know, since the road had been closed for a month during which time he had had to haul his produce through

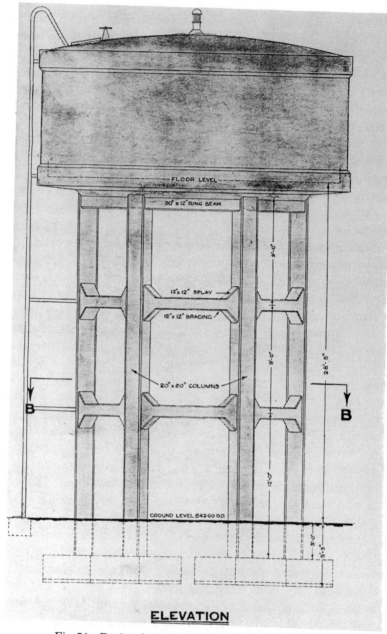

ELEVATION

Fig 56   Design for water tower at Martins Croft

the fields, who would be paying for the inconvenience and damage? A Mr W V Jenkins claimed £1 for damage to his garden and crops as a result of a trench being dug for a water main. After examination he was offered 12s 6d, without prejudice.

Harland Engineering Company supplied and erected one Ruston 5 HP engine, one Spiroglade centrifugal pump and one Lister vertical driving centrifugal booster pump. Quotations were received for insurance in the sum of £700 of the engines and plant in connection with the scheme over a five year period. The Municipal Mutual Insurance Ltd won hands down over the National Boiler and General Insurance Co Ltd with a quote £4 6s 9d cheaper than their rival – to wit £5 11s 2d. They were to report in 1937 that the insured plant appeared in good condition, receiving skilled and careful attention.

To support the installation, the aforementioned reservoir, or water tower, was built at the eastern end of Martins Croft. This was later augmented and eventually superseded by three steel tanks erected on the southern perimeter of the airfield. It was finally knocked down shortly before the commissioning in November 1986 of a handsome new 31-metre inverted conical concrete tower adjacent to the tanks. This now stands in competition with the church as Colerne's most conspicuous landmark!

Fig 57   New water tower and old tanks at west end of village

Half yearly charges were fixed for the domestic water supplies tied to the rateable value of the premises served, as in the following table:

RV	Charge		RV	Charge	
£ 8 or under	7s	4d	£15	12s	6d
9	8	0	16	13	4
10	8	4	17	14	0
11	9	4	18	14	10
12	9	10	19	15	10
13	10	10	20	16	6
14	11	4	above £20	5% of RV	

For each fixed bath and for each water closet exceeding one, 7s 6d would be levied; a motor car would be 10s! Non-domestic supplies would be charged 2s 3d per thousand gallons. These charges would be brought in from 1st December 1935.

There were small irritations such as a leaking hydrant causing loss of water for two or three days, but in the end the Engineers stated confidently that the supply would be available to the inhabitants of Colerne on and after 28th November. The Clerk cautiously had notices posted proclaiming water available on and after 30th November.

There was a spate of applications for water to be laid on from the new supply. Others were more hesitant and planned on continuing to use their wells; 7s 4d for six months' water might be 7s 4d they could ill afford. Outside interest was shown; the Editor of "The Oil Engine" wished to inspect the Widdenham installation with a view to writing an article about it in his journal. Water-wise, Colerne was now on the map.

From privy to sewage farm

It was not so with sewage. The saga of the sewage system, like the water one, goes back as far as there are records. There seemed always to have been complaints of nuisance, and worry about it polluting the drinking water – hence the constant harping on testing the water by the Ministry of Health during construction of the water system. Colerne Parish Council had complained yet again in 1937, on this occasion about the discharge of a sewer on Tutton Hill into an open ditch.

The RDC was galvanised into action, and by August of 1938 their Engineers had prepared a plan for outfall works at Watergates, to cost £7200. The check to this plan came from the Air Ministry, at that time building an aerodrome on the outskirts of Colerne. They proposed to discharge some 64,000 gallons of sewage per day into the Council's sewers. This drastically altered everything, since it meant the flow would be three times greater than the Council's proposals, and the cost of an enlarged scheme would put the price up to £12,860. Whilst the Council were deliberating whether they could face the increased cost the Second World War broke out and they were saved the trouble. The Air Ministry built their own works in 1940.

As in many rural areas, by the end of the war the problem of sewage disposal in Colerne, ironically exacerbated by the provision of piped water, was even more acute. Although the construction of the airfield system had contributed further to the delay, in the end, as we shall see, it also helped towards the solution of the problem.

In 1947 the RDC applied to the Ministry of Health to borrow £11,000 for "works and sewage disposal". An Inquiry was ordered and took place in the Meeting Room of the Six Bells, Colerne, starting at 10.30 am on 5th November 1947. Mr A Sheppard, Chairman of the Parish Council, said that they were aggrieved at the time at which the Inquiry was called, as it prevented those who were tied by their work from being able to attend and express their views. However, big guns were on their side: Dr Broomhead, the Medical Officer of Health, made an eloquent case for proceeding immediately with a proper scheme for the village. He said there were 99 properties with no system of drainage whatever, and a further 84 drained off to soakaways or ditches. Disposal was into swallow-holes (i.e. cavities in the lime-stone) or fissures, which was a potential pollution to water supplies, even some distance away. There were 155 earth closets and eleven privies, and it was impossible to dispose of the contents on the limited gardens; the result was that buckets had to be carried through the streets to the allotments, which he declared was a most insanitary practice. Since the installation of the water supply in 1935 the scheme had become more urgently necessary.

THE

PUBLIC HEALTH ACT, 1936,

AND THE

LOCAL GOVERNMENT ACT, 1933

COLERNE.

WHEREAS the Council of the Rural District of Calne and Chippenham have applied to the Minister of Health for consent to borrow the sum of £11,100 for works of sewerage and sewage disposal in the Parish of Colerne, and the Minister of Health has directed Inquiry into the subject-matter of such application.

NOTICE IS HEREBY GIVEN that V. D. JOLL, Esq., B.Sc., A.M.I.C.E., the Inspector appointed to hold the said Inquiry, will attend for that purpose at The Meeting Room, Six Bells, Colerne, Wilts, on Wednesday, the 5th day of November, 1947, at 10.30 o'clock in the Forenoon, and will then and there be prepared to receive the evidence of any persons interested in the matter of the said Inquiry.

A. TITHERLEY,
Assistant Secretary.

Ministry of Health,
October, 1947.

Printed by The Wilts Printing Works, Ltd., Chippenham.

Fig 58   Notice of meeting, 5th November 1947

COLERNE
SEWAGE DISPOSAL
Urgency of Scheme Stressed at Local Inquiry

" The present arrangements are inadequate, unsatisfactory and primitive," declared Dr. C. L. Broomhead, Medical Officer of Health to Calne and Chippenham Rural District Council, giving evidence at a Ministry of Health inquiry, conducted by Mr. A. A. L. Lane, at Colerne on Wednesday into the application of the District Council for a loan of £11,000 for purposes of sewerage and sewage disposal.

The Chairman of the Parish Council (Mr. A. Sheppard) emphasised the need for a sewerage scheme for the village, but said that to many of the villagers the inquiry seemed to be simply another means of delaying things a little bit longer. They were also aggrieved at the time at which the inquiry was called, as it prevented those who were tied by their work from being able to attend and express their views. The inhabitants were very concerned about it, and felt that immediate action should be taken.

Fig 59 *Wiltshire Times*, Saturday 8th November 1947

The Senior Sanitary Inspector, Mr E W Stevens, deplored the habit of pouring slop water into road gullies. One property in the rather congested village centre received his especial disapprobation, whilst admitting it was "futile to seek abatement because no practical suggestion could be offered as to ways and means of doing it". Mr T R Cox, the County Sanitary Inspector, said they were particularly anxious to get the school connected to the sewer.

Members of the public were also granted audience. Mrs Tiley, on behalf of the cottagers, said how essential the scheme was. She asked the Inspector to imagine the position in Colerne during the previous winter when the ground was frozen hard for several weeks. Miss Bird asked if Thickwood would be included, as it was becoming increasingly difficult in this agricultural area to get labour owing to the lack of sanitation.

It was "understood that the aerodrome would be occupied for an indefinite period" (no overstatement, since when the RAF departed the Army smartly moved in, and, in 1990, are still in residence!). A happier note was struck when it was revealed that the Air Ministry had agreed to sell their existing works to the Council for £2,500, thus significantly reducing the investment required to meet the needs of the village. This was just as well, as the RAF had 52 houses under construction, the RDC proposed erecting a further sixteen, and two private houses were in the offing. Applause followed when Mr Holton, Clerk to the RDC, said the Council had kept its promise, made during the war, that Colerne's should be the first post-war scheme.

The applause might not have been so hearty had those present realised that it was to be nearly fourteen months before the contractor, Ernest Ireland, was selected and enabled to commence. But from then on, in generally good weather, it went smoothly. The last surviving progress report, with completion in sight, is dated 3rd March 1950. However, it is recorded that some dwellings were not connected to the system, in particular the 52 new married quarters whose septic tanks were subsequently emptied into it. The next mention that appears, only six years after completion of the works, complains that the arrangements were already inadequate and proposes an increase in capacity at a total estimated cost of £13,800 (notice how the costs start to rise!). But it was argued in and outside the RDC Public Health Committee that the works were generally satisfactory and that relatively minor improvements would overcome the evident problems.

That, by and large, was the official line for the next quarter century. Minor improvements; new outfall from the works approved by the Minister in 1959; a ray of hope in '68 about the possible inclusion of an extension within a larger scheme for the District (no movement). But come the time that Forrester Green foul water sewers were adopted in September 1970, no further mention was made of the extension.

But, at last, in 1988 a proclamation by the Wessex Water Authority stated that the sewage discharged into the By Brook did not meet with national pollution standards. The works had finally failed to cope with the increased population of the expanding Colerne, hardly surprising since it barely coped in 1950! Now pumps, filters and tanks were to be improved in a programme costing half a million pounds. Mr Bryan Parker, head of WWA Public Affairs, said work would last until the spring of 1989, after which the effluent discharge should be of an acceptable standard.

So at last the work was put in hand; bigger cranes and diggers than ever seen before squeezed their way down Watergates just in time it seemed to save us from sewage running again in the streets; and, mercifully, in time to afford a happy ending to this vital chapter of our book on the history of our village.

Notes on Postal, Telegraph and Telephone Services in Colerne

Margaret Wood and Joyce Utting

The postal, telegraph and telephone system brought Colerne into contact with the outside world earlier and faster than roads and mechanical vehicles, other than the railway – but to use that entailed a goodly walk to Box.

The subject of communications will, we hope, be more fully explored in a further volume of Colerne history, but these notes trace the development of the Post Office services in the village.

Chippenham has always been the post town, though sometimes *via* Box. Colerne had its first post office in 1855. The Postmaster was Robert Bryant, a mason by trade, who lived in Tutton Hill. From 1857 until the late 1950s Colerne had its own postmark for franking mail.

Since 1855 the site of the Post Office has moved around, though never far from the High Street. The following is a list of the sites and the names of sub-Postmasters, Postmen and Postwomen from 1855 to 1990.

Sub-Postmasters and -Postmistresses

1855 to early 1860s
Robert Bryant, mason, Tutton Hill.

1860s to 1870s
John Gibbons, shop keeper, High Street.

1880s to 1910
Gideon May, shoemaker, Chapel Yard [Path] moved to the Post Office and bakery at the White Hart [2, Market Place]. The bakery was run by Samuel May.

Fig 60   Postcard showing Colerne postmark, 1905 (note halfpenny stamp)

1910–14
Cecil Dyer (son-in-law of Gideon May), building contractor, his business being in the Bath Road he lived in the Market Place when he was sub-Postmaster.

1914–19
Frederick Woodward, Post Office bakery and provision stores, Trunnalls Farm, High Street.

1919–38
Mrs Emma Woodward, wife of Frederick, as above.

1938–70
Vernon Notton, Post Office and grocery shop, Trunnalls Farm (so as not to confuse this with Trimnells Farm, Mr Notton used 20A High Street as the address).

1970–76
Mrs June Holder (now Mrs Bartlett), daughter of Mr Notton.

1976–86
Frank Jenkins, Post Office and grocery shop (the farm now being separate).

1986–
Richard Randall, the present sub-Postmaster. The grocery business is now closed.

Some Postmen and Postwomen

1861   George Green, a post messenger, was blind, lived in Thickwood.

1880   Gideon May, as above.

1940s Mrs Lena May, lived at 23, High Street.
Miss Emily Clark, lived at 36, High Street.

1956   Miss June Notton, who was supplied with a uniform, worked from 6 am to 10 am sorting and delivering mail to Bath Road, High Street, Tutton Hill and Watergates (other mail was delivered by van from Chippenham).

Until 1889 mail could only be posted at Colerne Post Office. In that year, however, a wall posting box was installed at Thickwood. There are now nine post boxes in and around the village.

Collections and deliveries were frequent and, for that reason, faster than the present service. The railways were used as the main carriers and fetching and delivering was done mostly on foot or with the aid of

Fig 61   Post Office in 1930s

Fig 62   Post Office, c1950

Fig 63   Post Office, 1990

a bicycle. Mail posted in the village in the morning would usually be delivered in the Chippenham–Bath area on the same day. We have been told by Ebenezer Knight that before 1914 there was a special 'perishable goods' service which meant that a joint of fresh pork could be posted from Colerne in the morning and delivered in Manchester that evening.

Telegraph and telephones

The telegraph service was available long before the telephone, and in 1903 Colerne became a telegraph office. Telegrams were sent and received with remarkable rapidity. Messages were tapped through from the receiving office to the appropriately equipped Post Office nearest to the recipient's address. They were written onto the telegram form and delivered by the telegraph boy, often on his bicycle, and very possibly by the late 1920s by motorcycle; however, we have no evidence at present that they were used in Colerne.

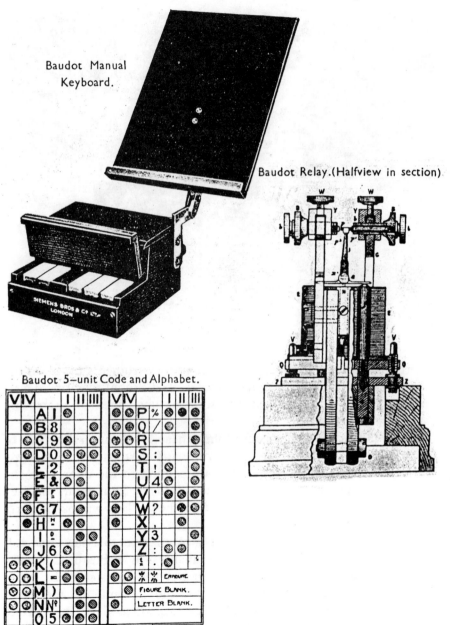

Fig 64   Telegraph transmitting machine used c1900

Fig 65   A telegraph delivery boy

Originally morse sounders or mechanical instruments based on the morse principle of dots and dashes were used. Rapid scientific development, however, produced transmitting machines of increasing sophistication.

Conan Doyle makes Sherlock Holmes heavily reliant on the speed of the telegraph service to solve his criminal investigations. For many people, the sight of the telegraph boy coming to the door with the yellow envelope in his hand struck fear into the household, for they were frequently used as the bearers of bad news. This was particularly so during the two world wars.

In 1903 Colerne Post Office was also enabled to issue and cash Money Orders, a service previously available only in Box or Corsham. This was a remarkable service. The money was transferred by using the telegraph system. The amount paid in and the name and address of the payee was telegraphed from the receiving office to the appropriate Money Order office. We are told that money could be collected as little as three hours after it had been deposited. It must have been a boon to families who were helped by money sent to them by sons and daughters working away from home.

Box telephone exchange opened in September 1907 and one of the first connections was Sir Alfred Read of Lucknam Park, telephone number Box 4. Even in 1939 there were only about twenty subscribers in the village and this included the Wiltshire Constabulary, the Post Office itself and a few commercial concerns. On 27th October 1914 a Call Office was connected to Bath telephone exchange and this was sited at the Post Office; this was, of course, the first public telephone service in the village. In 1915 Colerne had its own Telephonic Express Delivery Service.

In 1976 the Money Order Telegraph service was withdrawn from Colerne and centred in Box. In 1982 both this service and the telegram service were discontinued nationally.

Post Office at RAF Station, Colerne

From 1964 there has been a Post Office at RAF Colerne, now Azimghur Barracks, run by civilian Postmasters and Postmistresses. We have at present no information about the arrangements for mail or other Post Office services at the camp prior to this date. Printed here is a list of the people who have run the office since 1964 and some of the specific franking stamps which have been used (two of them to mark the Royal Air Force Association's Air Days). We have been told that this Post Office is housed in a building which was originally the fire station on the RAF camp.

Postmasters and Postmistresses

From 1964–January 1970
Mr Notton who also ran Colerne Post Office.

1st January 1970–8th November 1973
Mr S. Brisbane, 16, Fosseway Close, Colerne.

8th November 1973–8th March 1974
Mrs Brisbane, wife of the above, was the officer-in-charge.

8th March 1974–
Mr Paul Smith of Marshfield who is still the Postmaster, although his daughter Alison now runs the Post Office for him. Alison was assisted by Mrs Brisbane during the early 1980s.

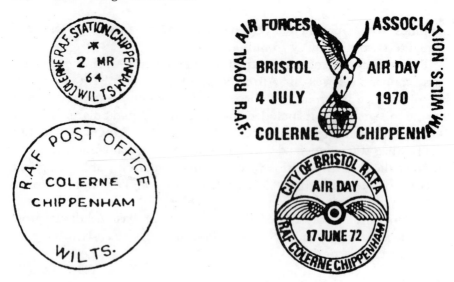

Fig 66   RAF Colerne postmarks

Sources

Ellis M J, *The Early History of the Telephone in Bath.*
Siggers J, *Wiltshire and its Postmarks.*
Bath Post Office Directories.
Kelly's Directories.
Archives of the Union of Communication Workers.